WEB OF LIES

MY LIFE WITH A NARCISSIST:

by Sarah Tate

with comment from Dr David Holmes

Web of Lies

Author's Disclaimer

"This autobiographical novel is based on my experiences over a ten-year period. Names have been changed, characters combined, and events compressed. Certain episodes are imaginative re-creation, and those episodes are not intended to portray actual events. Readers would do well to recognize that memory is, by nature, subjective, not objective."

Edited by C. A. Keller

ISBN-13: 978-1456516680

ISBN-10: 145651668X

Table of Contents

Depression, deceit and despair

Trapped in a spiders web

A Christmas from hell

Raw pain and emotion

Trying to gather strength

Truth hurts

Waking up, and taking action

This book is dedicated to my children.

And to Sofia

Prologue

She sat, in her empty house, only the dogs for company.

Alone, completely and utterly alone.

And where was he?

In another country, hundreds of miles away.

What was he doing? Working?

He told her he would be here, but at the last minute, work had interrupted his plans.

'Too much to do.'

He hadn't seen her in months, hadn't returned her calls, despite his promises.

She knew now.

He was gone.

Empty promises.

His words meant nothing.

She knew that now.

For the very first time, she saw her own destiny.

She'd fallen in love with a man who was devoid, empty, and hollow.

How could he do this do me?

He left me, alone and destitute.

Alone in this country.

Nobody to help.

No hope. Nothing…

She paced around the house.

Isolated, alone, desperate.

There it was, in the garage.

The wind was blowing, it was dark, and it was cold.

She found the answer, and she knew this was the only way.

A new century, a new millennium,

Out with the old…The only way to show him, maybe make him understand what he had done.

This would show him.

Poison, Rat poison. Anticoagulant.

I'll bleed to death Long and slow.

No more than I deserve.

A way out, but not just any way out.

This is a statement. A spectacular way out.

She picked up the bottle The dog, as always, at her side.

She walked back into the house.

This is it. Now or never.

'I'll show you. You bastard.'

She swallows ... and swallows ... and swallows...She fights the gagging sensation.

She holds the pillows; she realises her own despair.

It begins. It hurts.

Oh dear Jesus, how this hurts...

It starts The pain, the blood

The sorrow The loss The despair...

The love The forgiveness The sorrow...The pain,

The intense and all-consuming PAIN...

She bleeds She vomits

Then suddenly 'My family, my brother, my mother ...What am I doing?'

She fights, she tries to resist

But it's too late…She loses the fight, the life ebbs away, slowly but surely.

Her last thought: 'I hope you know what you did to me.'

'Why?'

'Oh why, dear Lord, why did you do this to me?'…

Chapter One

Swept Off My Feet

Extract from my journal: Feb 10th 2002.

*'Well, eighteen months later and boy did things happen in my
life !I'm getting married in three months, and the future is
looking bright for us! I've met the most wonderful man on the
planet, and he wants me to be his wife! I can't believe it,
really I can't! How things can turn around so quickly! I'm so
happy and full of hope! This is the turning point formed. I
love him so much and I'm so lucky to have him!'*

I am Sarah, and I was twenty-nine years old when I made the
decision to leave my hectic life in Berlin for a gentler way of
life in Switzerland. It was a big decision to make, and
certainly one that would turn my life both upside down and
inside out. I'd always had this idea I'd end up with an older
man. I don't know why, or where it came from. I'd had
plenty of failed relationships with men around my own age,
so I guess I just decided I needed somebody older and wiser.
My life before had been hectic, fast, and even heinous. I'd
spent my twenties living the party life. Work hard and party
harder, that was my ethos. It had been great, but it had come
at a price. By the time I hit twenty-nine I knew it was time
for a big change. I needed to slow down. Perhaps this was
where the idea of the older man was born in my psyche. Born
from the knowledge that things must change: born from a
desire to live a 'normal' and 'stable' life. It had all happened
so quickly I barely had time to register it. From making the

decision to leave my current job and the big city behind, to finding myself on a plane to a new country and a new life, it seemed barely a heartbeat had passed. Yet there I was, suddenly in a new land, full of new people and new promise. The contrast could not have been greater. I moved from a life in the big smoke, to life in the countryside. From all weekend 'benders', to farming landscapes and peaceful church chimes. How happy I was with my decision!

And then, before my suitcase was even unpacked (my furniture was still in transit!), there he was. We met in our place of work. I was the latest addition to the Procurement team; he was the manager of a small department over in Marketing. From the moment he walked through the door of his office (he was late that day, and I was already there, talking to a colleague) his attention focused solely on me. He immediately engaged me in conversation, completely ignoring the gentleman I was actually there to see. We spent about thirty minutes talking about me, when I'd arrived, how I was finding the new job. His attention was so fixed on me I remember feeling slightly awkward. Who was this stranger who had interrupted my meeting? I wondered what it was he wanted from me. Physically, Bill made no impact on me whatsoever. He was short, overweight and balding. Worst of all, from my point of view, he was smoking a cigarette. At that point he had (so he told me) a twenty a day habit, yet from that day onwards, I never saw him smoke another cigarette.

In an effort to shift both his attention and the focus of the conversation away from myself, I asked him about his job, his department, and what his role in the company was. He seized on this opportunity to immediately arrange a 'meeting' with him the next morning so that we could discuss this in 'more detail'. I agreed. I wasn't busy at that time, and I welcomed the opportunity, on a professional level, to be introduced to his department. The next day, I duly attended the 'meeting', only to find it was just between Bill and me. Instead of outlining his department's function, he sat me down at his PC and called up a map of the local area. He then proceeded to explain in great detail where all the best restaurants and shops were located. He talked about his social life; which customers he regularly entertained, where he entertained them, and which wine is served in which restaurant. By the time he had finished his speech, it was conveniently lunchtime, so he suggested we go to the local Italian, where he'd treat me to pizza. As it was Friday, and my new boss was abroad on business, I gladly accepted. I felt comfortable with Bill, as he was so very attentive. I was at ease, but nothing more. At that point he was still just a friendly manager who was happy to show the new girl on the block the way around. By the end of lunch, though, something had changed. I don't know if it was the red wine he insisted I drink, or the never-ending rhetoric and humour. He had me laughing and chatting, and most of all relaxing. By the time he dropped me back off at my office, we had arranged to meet that evening in a local hotel for drinks. I had a strange tingling feeling in my stomach. I felt somehow elated. I smiled for the rest of the afternoon.

* * *

As I got ready that evening there was no thought in my mind that this would be a romantic liaison. I did not fancy Bill one bit. I was, however, extremely happy to be meeting him for this date, because he made me feel so comfortable. I thought he would be a great friend to have, somebody who was the life and soul, loved by all. I was flattered by the attention he'd shown me, yet I naively believed he was simply a nice man who wanted to do me a favour. I convinced myself he wouldn't want anything romantic from me anyway. I was seventeen years younger than he was, and already it was clear to me that he was intellectually out of my league. I didn't think for a second that a man in his position would make a move on me. He was obviously a man of means, and highly intelligent. I was impressed by his command of the language, his knowledge of politics and the arts (all things which were alien to me, as I'd spent the last ten years sitting in night clubs talking nonsense to nobodies!). I was fascinated by his tales and couldn't wait to spend more time with him.

We met at a lake front five star hotel. He was there before me and had already 'taken the liberty' of ordering our wine. During the course of that first evening he bought two bottles of one of the most expensive wines on the menu. For a girl who was used to sipping Becks beer from the bottle, this was really quite something. From the hotel bar we moved to a small nightclub in the basement, where the drinks continued to flow. We exchanged tales of our respective pasts, and he told me that he'd been married twice. His first marriage had taken place when he was very young and naïve, his second marriage was one of business convenience. It was a mutual agreement between himself and a friend (who happened to also be his accountant).He told me he had three adult children by his first wife: no offspring from the second marriage.

I was fascinated, spellbound. This man had led a full and colourful life. He was well-travelled, well-versed, and so very experienced. Not only that, but he was clearly a successful businessman, who had 'retired' to his position in the company where we worked, in order to 'kick back and enjoy life' a little more. I wondered what on earth it was that Bill could possible find interesting about little old me. Here I was, just twenty-nine, and with no significant story to tell, and yet he seemed in awe of me. The perfect gentleman, he appeared genuinely interested in everything I had to say. He paid me compliments, held open doors, and treated me with kindness and respect. As the evening wore on, I was becoming more and more drunk, and I was having an absolutely fantastic time. It certainly seemed as though Bill was too, because when it came time to leave the club, it was clear that neither of us wanted to leave the other's company just yet.

"Why don't we go back to mine?" he suggested.

"I don't know about you, but I'm starving, and I think we both need some food to help mop up all this wine!"

I had to agree. Once out in the fresh air I was staggering somewhat. Not really a good look when you're on a first date with somebody, but I felt so completely comfortable in his company by now, it really didn't seem to matter. I gladly accepted his invitation, comfortable that he really was a perfect gentleman, and that we were going to become the best of friends. That was the start of the weekend that would change the course of my entire life.

* * *

I woke up in the morning with my head spinning. At first I didn't even know where I was. I looked around the room. I was in Bill's bedroom, lying in bed fully clothed. I remembered him leading me here a few hours earlier. For a split second I felt panic, did I...?

Then I heard him moving around in the kitchen, and I realised he had let me use his bed, and had slept on the sofa.

"Good morning Sarah! You look like you need a coffee!"

"Morning Bill... .Ouch ... yes, coffee would be nice please."

He was bright and breezy, and incredibly funny. I felt once again at ease, if a little perplexed and extremely hung over.

7

"So, what shall we do today? How about I take you out and show you some of the sights? What would you like to do, name anything, we'll do whatever you want."

I couldn't really think straight. I hadn't planned on spending today with him as well, but when I thought about it, what else did I have to do? My furniture had still not arrived, so I was literally camping in my new flat. A day of sightseeing with Bill sounded like fun.

"Actually Bill, I fancy getting some exercise to blow the cobwebs away a bit."

"Perfect! Great idea! Do you swim? I know a lovely hotel with a spa, how about that for blowing cobwebs away?"

"That sounds like a fantastic idea, Bill," I smiled. This was going to be a great weekend. As he was handing me a coffee, my mobile phone rang. It was my mum. He indicated to me that he was going to take a shower. I took the call and moved out to the balcony so I could speak to her. I didn't want her knowing I'd just spend the night with a man (albeit not 'with' him), and I couldn't face having to explain it. I'd only arrived in my new town a week or so ago, and I thought she'd probably start worrying if she knew I'd already started to get close to a man.

Whilst I was on the balcony, Bill suddenly put his head around the door; he was naked except for a towel. He proceeded to speak to me despite, knowing I was talking to my mother. I shot him a nervous look, which made him stop talking as he made one of those 'oops' faces. She heard his voice, and immediately asked me who it was.

"Oh, it's a friend from work who has offered to take me into town today. He's just arrived to pick me up," I lied. We went to a beautiful spa hotel on the banks of the lake. There was a small swimming pool and a Jacuzzi area. We leapt in the Jacuzzi and laughed with excitement. I was having an absolute ball. Bill ordered drinks from the bar. Bloody Mary's. I'd never had a Bloody Mary in my life. More alcohol!

* * *

At this stage we had the pool area completely to ourselves. It was a cold October Saturday morning after all; not many people were about. As the drinks were delivered Bill was just getting out of the pool. I walked over to the sun lounger area and lay down on one, a warm, fuzzy, and very contented feeling in my stomach. Once the waiter had gone, Bill was standing at the foot of my sun lounger. Suddenly, and for no apparent reason, he took down his swimming trunks. He was standing right in front of me, full frontal. I didn't know where to look! We were in a public place after all, and he must surely have known it was completely inappropriate to simply disrobe like he did.

"What are you doing?" I exclaimed.

"What's wrong?" He asked innocently, standing there confidently.

"In my family we always walked naked in front of each other, there's nothing wrong with it!"

"We're not family, and we're not in a family home!" I was mortified by now, but I brushed it aside. As he replaced his swimmers and handed me my drink, I laughed it off.

Looking back now I can see that 'this incident', on my very first date with him, compared with the phone incident earlier in the day, were classic signs of Bill asserting his dominance. To attempt to put a stamp on something which is yours is classic narcissistic behaviour. Events like this were to happen many more times over the coming months and years.

Chapter Two

Tales From the Past

By the end of that first weekend I was in a complete daze. It wasn't that 'bowled over' daze you get when you have been knocked off your feet and swept away with the first throes of passion. It was more a state of pleasant confusion, slight bewilderment, and nervous anticipation. Bill had been the perfect gentleman all weekend, yet we seemed to have become incredibly close, incredibly quickly. Sunday in particular had been full of deep and meaningful conversations, in which he'd revealed tome some fascinating yet largely disturbing facts about his past life. There was no doubt that this man had lived a lot in his forty-seven years. I was in awe of his achievements and deeply intrigued by his complicated and intricate love life. He hadn't talked a great deal about his first wife during that first weekend except to reiterate that he had married her out of lust; explaining that he was very young as if this were some sort of excuse. He told me that she was a couple of years older than him and they had met whilst he was very briefly in the RAF. She was a devout Catholic, and as he so eloquently put it, he 'wanted to get into her pants' which is why he'd proposed. Six years and three children later, the marriage had 'irretrievably broken down' despite Bill's best efforts. He explained that he'd worked his fingers to the bone, taking on several jobs simultaneously in order to keep their heads financially above water but that nothing he had done had been enough to satisfy his then wife. He had desperately wanted to keep things together for the sake of the children, two girls and a boy, yet nothing would work. He said he had felt desperate when his wife had refused to speak to him altogether, choosing instead to communicate only through the eldest child. Bill explained that this had broken his heart, as he felt his child was being manipulated into an unbearable position by her mother, and he said he felt the only way to alleviate the problem would be to leave. At that stage, we didn't talk much more about what had happened after the marriage had failed. Bill just told me that he had maintained a relationship with his children, but from a distance. This, he said, had been an incredibly painful thing for him, but he knew it was best for the children, as he really hadn't wanted them caught in the crossfire between himself and their mother. Even though I barely knew him, I concluded that he must be an incredibly honourable man, who had sacrificed his own needs in order to ensure that his children were protected from the bitter divorce and the acrimony between himself and his first wife (which had mostly come from her side, he said).

The disturbing part came when Bill explained to me what had happened to his second wife, Sofia. He told me that they had got married ten years previously, but that the marriage had been purely one of convenience. They were business partners, very good friends, and they had settled down together as a way of getting around the tax laws in Germany where he was running a business at the time. Sofia was German, and his marriage to her enabled him to profit from lower tax breaks. He was adamant that their relationship was platonic, and even went so far as to describe to me the one and only occasion they had ever consummated the marriage. This apparently happened after a drunken party, and Bill was quick to tell me he was quite repulsed by the episode. He said that Sofia's 'smell' was all wrong for him, but he felt sometimes that maybe she had wanted or hoped for more from the relationship. He maintained, however, that she was content with their arrangement and the lavish lifestyle his profitable business supplied her with. He explained that despite their strong friendship, things had started to unravel between them once Bill's business in Germany had closed and the couple moved to the South of France together.

Towards the end of the 1990's it was clear the marriage was coming to an end. In 1997 Bill told me he had decided to come to Switzerland to make a new life for himself, whilst Sofia remained at the marital home in France. Bill then explained that during the final twelve months, he and Sofia had drifted further and further apart, but had remained on speaking terms. Bill had suspected that Sofia had started to fall into a depression in 1999when the subject first came up of them formally ending the marriage. Despite the dip, Bill had assumed that Sofia was getting her life back together. He told me she had opened a small bookstall on the local market in France, and that he suspected she even had a new man in her life. Bill told me that towards the end of 1999, they had mutually decided that the best thing for everybody would be if they were to divorce. He told me that by then he believed she was in another relationship anyway, and that the best thing would be to separate. That way they could both concentrate on their new lives, his in Switzerland and hers in France. He explained that over the Christmas period of 1999 he had spoken to Sofia on several occasions and that she had seemed fine and in good spirits. He said he'd been helping her to try to fix a computer problem. For some reason he had decided to work over the entire Christmas and New Year's Holiday of that year. He explained that he had returned home from work on January 4th 2000 to find the police on his doorstep. They told him that his family in France had been trying to reach him, and that something dreadful had happened. That very same day he raced all the way down to France, having been told by his Father (who also lived in France) that Sofia had taken her own life. Once he arrived in France he was told by the police that Sofia had most likely taken her life on Millennium Eve, but had lain undiscovered for three days. I asked him how she'd taken her life, and he revealed that she had swallowed rat poison. As he relayed these details to me he was shaking, and at this point my heart just went out to him for what he'd been through. He explained in detail how he'd had to go into the house where she'd lain, in order to clear up the mess which was left in the bedroom where she'd taken her life. He described to me the mess on the walls and in the bed. He cried as he recalled throwing the soiled mattress through the open window and later having to burn it in the garden. He told me he'd never experienced anything so traumatic in his life, and I certainly believed him. I couldn't stop thinking about poor Sofia and how she'd ended her life, and the effect it must have had on poor Bill. I asked Bill if he believed Sofia had killed herself because she knew the marriage was coming to a close, but he said he really didn't believe so, because despite agreeing to end the marriage, the two of them had remained on really good terms. He went on to explain that whilst he'd been sorting through Sofia's belongings, he had actually come across a suicide note which she had written to her mother a decade earlier. He said he couldn't recall the details of the letter, but that to him it confirmed that Sofia had always been of unstable mind, as she had clearly contemplated killing herself on at least one occasion before.

That Sunday night, as Bill relayed this story to me, I put my arms around him. I held him for quite some time as he was shaking and sobbing. At this moment I felt an overwhelming sense of pride that he'd taken me into his confidence in this way, and had shown me his vulnerable side. I vowed then to always be there for Bill, and be the best friend I could possibly be to him. All I wanted to do in that moment was to help him. I felt incredibly close to him in his moment of vulnerability, and I knew deep down that I was also starting to fall for this man in a big way.

The end of that first weekend with Bill signalled the start of a complete whirlwind in my life. The next few weeks, Bill never left my side. Wherever I went, he accompanied me. He took me to expensive restaurants and posh hotels, day trips sightseeing and wonderful evenings in front of his open fireplace. He cooked for me and boy, could the man cook! He sang to me, and he wrote poetry for me; he wrote letters to me. He lavished me with expensive gifts despite my protests; he indulged my every need and desire. It was impossible to resist. I was in seventh heaven. It was everything I'd ever dreamed of. It was paradise. I'd honestly never felt so happy in my life. Even during the day, when we were at work, he sent me email after email. It must have been about ten a day and they were long ones too. I often wondered how on earth he ever actually managed to do any work at all. He was supposed to be a manager after all.

"When do you work?" I'd ask, after just receiving yet another long and poetic Email.

"Oh, for me this is not a problem. The job is but a pastime. I'm here only to delegate. They pay me good money for nothing. I have a brain the size of a planet, after all."

He loved to quote 'Hitchhiker's Guide to the Galaxy'. He likened himself to Marvin the Paranoid Android constantly. Back then, I found it amusing. I didn't see him as flippant or arrogant in the slightest. I was completely spellbound. To me, he really did have a brain the size of a planet. I was completely and utterly in awe of him. To read his emails, listen to his soft voice, hear him singing and playing the guitar for me, reading his poetry; all this simply transported me away to another place, a place where only Sarah and Bill existed. I didn't want to be with anybody else. Within weeks, it was a general assumption amongst all my new friends, and anybody else that I met, that Bill and I had become a couple. Many people seemed to believe that we had been together for some time, and he was actually the reason I had moved to Switzerland. The relationship was moving so fast, I suppose I forgave people for drawing this conclusion, although if anybody asked me, I always made sure to put them right. I had come here on my own, and only met Bill subsequently. I'm not sure everybody believed that though.

He'd had a girlfriend, you see. He told me he'd started seeing her when he was in turmoil over Sofia's death earlier that year. It was a romance on the rebound. After I'd known him for about three weeks, she travelled from her home in Ireland to visit him, and he tried to end their relationship during her trip. She'd cut the visit short and returned home. A few days later I was with him by the lakeside and he'd received a call from her. They spoke for just a minute or so when she suddenly called him 'a bastard' then hung up. He explained to me that he felt awful. Clearly this woman had fallen for him, and had even been making plans to give up her life in Ireland and move to Switzerland to be with him. As soon as he'd met me, she'd been dropped. To be honest, at the time I didn't give her too much thought. It was selfish of me, I know. But by then I was under his spell, and I didn't want anything or anybody to come between us. I deliberately put it out of my mind.

Two months into the relationship, Bill and I were planning to spend our first Christmas together. He took me into town one day, to an expensive department store. There he led me to the Christmas section, and asked me to pick out all the decorations for 'our' tree, in his apartment. I was like a child

17

in a sweet shop. Money was clearly no object (I'd known this for some time) so I indulged and bought every decoration I'd ever dreamed of buying in my previous life. We decorated his apartment, went out together to choose our tree, brought it home and set to work. He lit the fire, put on some classical Christmas music and we planned our festive season together.

I was on cloud nine, and not for one second did I even dream to consider what had been happening in Bill's life just twelve months previously. Not once did I spare a thought for Sofia and what she had been going through this time last year. When I look back now, I wonder why on earth it didn't occur to me then. As time went by, I would spend more and more time preoccupied with Sofia, her life with Bill, and her subsequent demise. But at that moment in time, it was just about Bill and me. I was relishing the attention and love I was receiving. I'd never felt so adored by a man. I was starting to think all my birthdays and Christmases had come at once. And for him it was clearly the same. He repeatedly told me that I was his 'soul mate,' the woman he'd been waiting his entire life to meet. Nobody he'd been with before could ever compare to me. I was the one, and he wanted to be with me for the rest of his life.

Chapter Three

A Fairytale Romance

By March 2001 we had moved into our very first home together, a gorgeous maisonette apartment close to Lake Lucerne and a stone's throw from the cable car to the local ski resort. Life was amazing. My relationship with Bill was unlike any I'd ever had before. He really was my very best friend. I felt I needed nobody except him.

At the beginning of the year I'd travelled to Berlin to visit some friends. I had been away for just a couple of nights, yet when he picked me up at the airport upon my return, he was overcome with emotion.

"I never want to spend another night away from you; it was torture not having you with me."

His words almost moved me to tears, and I knew then that I too didn't want to spend another night away from him. My thirtieth birthday was fast approaching, and I knew Bill was planning something special. One Saturday he took me into town to one of the top designer shops, and asked me to choose a 'special occasion' dress. With his help and guidance I chose a luxury black evening gown. He then took me to a lingerie shop, where together we selected new (and very expensive) underwear. From there he took me into a jeweller's shop, and when he led me up to the counter the salesman immediately knew him by name.

"Turn away now," said Bill with a smile as he grabbed my left hand and thrust it towards the shop assistant. My face turned crimson as I realised what was happening.

"Pretend you're somewhere else!" laughed Bill. I giggled like a silly schoolgirl as the shop assistant measured my ring finger.

* * *

The weekend of my Birthday arrived and I was treated to a luxurious breakfast in bed. I knew we were going to a hotel, but I still didn't know where exactly. We caught the steamboat from the ferry station close to where we lived. We travelled first class (as we always did these days) and had a champagne lunch on our way to Lucerne. Once in town we caught a taxi up the mountain to the luxury Chateau Gütsch Hotel. I couldn't believe it when we checked into the Presidential Suite! I knew I was to be treated like royalty, Bill always treated me like a Princess, but this really surpassed anything we'd done before.

Once in the room Bill opened another bottle of champagne and started to fill the Jacuzzi. I strolled out onto the terrace and stood staring at the spectacular view of Lucerne, the lake, and the beautiful Alps beyond. I was in heaven. We took a Jacuzzi together and spent the rest of the afternoon in bed. It was probably one of the first times we'd truly made love. Our love life had been somewhat stilted until that point. Despite Bill's amazing overconfidence in every other aspect of his life, he'd always seemed to lack confidence in the bedroom.

Today was different though. Today he was in his element in every way. In the early evening Bill suggested we get ready for our meal in the hotel restaurant. I showered and carefully got ready in my new designer underwear, dress, and shoes. As I stood in this luxury bathroom, applying my make-up, I was completely blown away by how much my life had changed in such a short time. I really was a Princess in a Castle. This was the stuff of fairy tales.

The evening was beautiful, and as I emerged from the bathroom Bill took me by the hand and led me back onto the terrace to watch the sunset. By this stage we were both incredibly nervous, as we both knew what was about to happen. For the very first time, I saw Bill lose some of his cockiness; he was genuinely nervous about what he was about to do.

"Sarah, you've changed my life. I cannot thank you enough. I knew the moment I saw you that you were the one for me. You are beautiful, and I want to spend the rest of my life with you. Please, do me the honour of becoming my wife."

With that, we both dissolved into fits of giggles.

"Aren't you going to get down on one knee?"

I laughed. So he did, and with that he produced the ring, and my life was complete.

* * *

Two weeks later we were in the UK to let my family know the good news. My parents were genuinely pleased for me. Despite the age gap and Bill's prior history, my parents gave us their blessing. They could see how happy I was, and if they did have any reservations, they kept them quiet.

My mum and I have always been very close, and we'd discussed Bill's history at length. She agreed with me that Bill's life had been tough, he'd had some really bad luck, but he seemed completely genuine and besotted with me.

"We need to pick a venue," Bill had said just before we left for the UK.

"What sort of thing do you have in mind?"

I hadn't really thought about it too much. I knew I wanted to have all my close friends at the wedding, and that I wanted a nice 'traditional' dress, but beyond that I really didn't know. One day at work, I got an Email from him with a link in it. It was for a Castle in North Yorkshire, which had recently acquired a civil ceremony license. It looked amazing! A Castle!!

"Let's go and take a look at it while we're there," he said. I was so excited! The venue was spectacular; it was everything a bride-to-be dreams of. An old Castle set in acres of grounds, fantastic views of the Yorkshire countryside, and a small guest house next door for guests who would be travelling from far afield. I loved it; it was like a dream come true.

"Let's book it!" he said.

"What? Now? You want to book it now?" I exclaimed.

"Sure, why not!"

We picked a date approximately twelve months ahead. We signed on the dotted line, and the deposit was paid. It didn't even occur to me to ask Bill how he was going to pay for it. He clearly had lots of money at his disposal. I knew roughly what his salary was, and I realised he must have other money as well, because our lifestyle was fairly extravagant and money had never been an issue. I assumed Bill had made lots of money from his previous business, the one he'd run with Sofia. He had intimated to me that he owned property in both France and Germany, and he'd explained that he had a significant amount of money in an offshore account, which he regularly used to top up his salary.

* * *

When we moved in together I had insisted (against Bill's wishes) that I pay half of the rent on our apartment. Despite knowing he had money, and gratefully accepting the gifts and the lifestyle he liked to provide me with, I was still extremely keen to pay my own way. I was earning good money myself then, so between us our disposable income was well above average.

When we returned to Switzerland, a big announcement was made and Bill organised all our friends and work colleagues to attend an engagement party at a bar in town. In true Bill

style the drinks were on him for the entire night. No expense
was spared, and as usual I was in seventh heaven. It was
around this time that Bill started talking to me about a project
he was working on with the company. He'd been spending a
lot of time with some Japanese clients, making several trips
to Tokyo before I'd met him, and entertaining the clients on
their trips to Switzerland. He mentioned several times that
the Japanese clients were interested in employing him, and
asked me if I would be interested in starting a new life in
Japan. At that point, I didn't care where I went, as long as it
was with Bill, and the offer they seemed to be making him
certainly appeared attractive. Bill always impressed on me
how much money he was 'worth' in terms of work.

"If we were to go to Japan, I'd work as a consultant and
wouldn't even consider doing it for less than one thousand
pounds sterling per day. That would be the minimum."

I was always amazed at the sums of money he was able to
command. To me, one thousand pounds per day was beyond
comprehension. But Bill was an incredibly intelligent and
highly educated man, with a wealth of experience. He wasn't
modest about it either, he liked people to know how clever he
was and how much money he earned. He would always make
a point of mentioning it to people at every opportunity.
According to Bill, he'd left the RAF after just two years,
aged twenty-one, and had then gone on to work in numerous
academic jobs. He'd studied maths, taking a degree at the
Open University, and he'd also found time to study for a
degree in Aerospace Engineering. All this whilst working

24

three jobs and teaching night school, all to put food on the table for his first three children. He kept repeating his favourite Hitchhiker's Guide to the Galaxy quote, 'I have a brain the size of a planet', and I for one really believed this to be true.

* * *

When he wasn't talking about Japan, he was talking about France. Bill owned a property in the South of France, and it was here that he had always wanted to retire. He told me he'd felt spiritually connected to this part of the world for many years, and it was for this reason he'd bought a small run-down farmhouse there, with a view to renovating it and retiring there. The house had stood empty for some time, until the mid-nineties when Bill's father and stepmother had moved into it. Bill had explained to me that he'd allowed his parents to live in the house rent free, in return for them maintaining it.

Not long after the engagement, Bill and I decided to make our first journey to France. I knew this would be a very tough visit for Bill, as it was to be his first time returning there since Sofia's death. After her death, her belongings had been stored in the cellar of a friend's house, and Bill had decided the time had now come to retrieve some belongings and organise the removal of the remainder of her stuff, so as not to be a burden on the friends any more. I wasn't looking forward to the trip. I was worried about meeting Sofia's friends. The couple we would be staying with had known her well. It was the women who had actually found Sofia's body after she'd called around to check on her over the Millennium. The discovery had affected her so much she was still in therapy almost eighteen months later. Bill was more blasé about the trip. He was confident that his friends would welcome me with open arms, despite my reservations that it was very soon after Sofia's death. I wondered what they would make of me and my relationship with Bill. I was acutely aware of not wanting to cause any offense to these people, but Bill seemed oblivious.

"They're my friends. They want me to be happy," he said, but still I felt uneasy. We drove through the night and arrived at Bill's friends' place at seven a.m. on a Sunday morning.

"You can't call them now!" I said.

"They have a young daughter. We can't get them out of bed so early on a Sunday!"

"Why not?" he said incredulously.

"They're my friends! Relax!" And so we knocked on their door at seven a.m., and from the moment they answered it, you could have cut the atmosphere with a knife. The husband was pleasant enough to both Bill and me, but the wife could barely bring herself to look at me. She spoke to Bill but was very reserved, and I wondered why he didn't seem to pick up on the atmosphere. I kept my left hand out of sight and prayed silently that Bill wouldn't mention that we were engaged. It all felt so wrong! I could feel their disapproval of

26

our relationship, and I could certainly understand how bad it must have looked. Here was Bill, making his first return to France since Sofia's suicide, and he brings a much younger new fiancé with him! No wonder they had their doubts!

Our stay with them dragged, and the reason for our stay proved equally as traumatic. I hadn't really been prepared for being confronted with the person herself. Until this point I'd only heard talk of her. Bill didn't even have a picture. Yet here I was, surrounded by the remnants of her life, and she suddenly became very real to me. If I'm honest, I was quite taken aback when I saw her belongings. Bill had always given me the impression they were a wealthy partnership, and given his penchant for designer gear and 'only the best' purchasing mentality, I think I'd expected to find a wealth of glamour and glitz. Not so. Sofia's belongings were sparse, worn, and sorry looking. The clothes were faded and old; books were worn and tattered. I felt very sad going through it all, because as I did, I started to get a picture of the woman and how she had lived. It certainly hadn't been glamorous. At this point though, I assumed that she had chosen to live this way. She clearly didn't share Bill's materialistic tendencies, choosing rather to live a quiet life with fewer possessions. In many ways I admired this. Bill wasn't unmoved by what we were doing. I thought he was being incredibly strong, under what I assumed were incredibly difficult circumstances. It appeared to me that he was less interested in Sofia's belongings and keener to sort through the business documents from their German company. I assumed looking through Sofia's things was too painful for him. He spent a great deal of time checking the paperwork, which to me looked like old documents and receipts, certainly nothing of any interest. I left it entirely up to Bill to decide which items he wanted to remove and take back home to Switzerland. I didn't feel it was my place to even suggest anything. To me, it just didn't seem right. Eventually we loaded the car with various items of furniture, some stereo equipment, mountain bikes and other knick-knacks. Bill's friends then agreed to dispose of the rest of the belongings. I think they just wanted us out of the house, to be honest, and I was certainly glad when the time came to leave. From there we drove to Bill's country house, where we were to enjoy a much more pleasant stay with his parents.

* * *

That evening, after enjoying several glasses of wine and whilst sitting in the garden looking out at the view of the French countryside, Bill finally cracked. He didn't speak about what had happened, he just stared into the distance and cried. I assumed that the day had really got to him, and that seeing Sofia's belongings piled up in a cellar like that had really been just too much to handle. I sat on his knee and held him as he wept for Sofia, and I wept with him. I was glad to return to Switzerland and get away from her ghost, for the time being at least.

* * *

However, not long after we returned from that trip, Bill received an Email from his friend, telling him he would not be welcome in their home any more, that the friendship was over. I was horrified. I thought it must be my fault! They disapproved of Bill's relationship with me. In many ways I could totally understand this, and I felt awful. Bill said it was because his friend's wife was 'screwed up' about finding Sofia's body, and had decided to blame him for everything which had gone wrong in Sofia's life. He was reticent about the Email and, despite my request that he try to clear the air with his friends, he never contacted them again.

Chapter Four

A Hint of Things to Come

Six months before the big day, and the wedding preparations were in full swing. The venue was booked, the guest list drawn up. Bill even setup a website for our friends so they could keep up to date with the latest news. No expense was to be spared. We'd organised flowers, cars, dresses, a great big cake, the works. This was going to be my fairytale dream wedding, and I was so excited and happy.

In autumn 2001 Bill whisked me away to another luxury hotel on the shores of Lake Geneva. We spent a glorious weekend having spa treatments, sipping champagne and making love. Bill always insisted that I wear the best clothes and jewellery. He often bought me things that weren't to my taste at all, but I'd wear them because I really wanted to please him. When we were dining out or staying in posh hotels, I knew that Bill always felt very proud of me and the way I looked. I always felt proud to be with him as well, because wherever we went in the early days, he would always draw attention to me, telling me in front of others how beautiful I was, and how proud he was that I was his fiancé. Who wouldn't be flattered by that sort of attention? Then, in October 2001, the first cloud appeared on the otherwise flawless horizon. Bill received registered mail from a debt collecting company in Zürich. Inside was a demand for roughly three hundred thousand Swiss francs.

At first he wouldn't tell me what it was, but as I knew something was seriously wrong he finally explained. He appeared to be completely in shock at the demand and said he didn't even know what it was and why he was receiving it. He went to the company lawyer to get some confidential advice, and explained to me afterwards that he believed the money had been borrowed by Sofia using the company they owned in Germany. The loan was from a German bank. I was absolutely horrified. I couldn't believe that Bill's wife had borrowed that much money without him even knowing about it!

"Well what did she borrow it for?" I asked him.

"I have no idea," he said, shaking his head.

"But surely you must have known? You must have signed something!"

"I signed lots of things; she was the company accountant and I trusted her."

"So you mean she put loan documents in front of you, and you signed them without even knowing? She tricked you into borrowing the money?"

"Like I said, I signed lots of things. She even had a signature stamp with my name on. I knew nothing about this loan."

"Oh my God! Well what the hell are we going to do then?"

"Relax, Sarah, this isn't your problem. I'll sort it! I'll either pay it, or I'll just declare myself bankrupt!"

"You'll declare yourself bankrupt? Oh my God!" I was utterly devastated; we hadn't even got married yet and he was talking about declaring himself bankrupt!

"Well, can you afford to pay it?" I asked

"Yes, I can. I don't want to pay it. I don't see why I should; this money wasn't borrowed by me or for me, I'd rather go bankrupt than pay it. We can put everything into your name. Please relax! I'll sort it!"

I tried to relax but it wasn't easy. I couldn't stop thinking about Sofia and why she would go behind Bill's back like that. What on earth did she do with the money? Was this the reason she had committed suicide? I couldn't stop thinking about it. Why had she betrayed him like that? And why didn't she try talking to him about it rather than take her own life?

Bill ignored that first demand for money, and for several months, things returned to normal. It remained in the back of my mind, but whenever I questioned Bill I got the same reply, 'Please relax, I'm taking care of it', so, in my naivety, I assumed he knew what he was doing. Around about the same time, Bill came home from work one day looking forlorn.

"What's the matter?" I asked.

"It's Sofia again," he said, shaking his head.

"I had a bank account in Germany for each of my kids. I gave her the bank books and asked her to organise a transfer each month into each account from my company in Germany. She was always in control of all the money, and she had the bankbooks in her possession. When we went to France I picked up the books, and I recently sent them to a friend in Germany to take them to the bank and update them. They've just comeback. All three accounts are empty. There was never any money paid into them at all."

"What??" I was incredulous.

"How much money was she supposed to deposit each month?"

"Five hundred Euros, per child, per month......for ten years."

"What? And she didn't deposit ANY of it?"

"Nope, it seems not." Bill looked close to tears.

"So basically you're telling me she stole from you and your kids for the entire duration of your relationship?" Bill nodded. I went over and held him. I couldn't believe what I was hearing. He'd married her and given her so much: provided for her; given her such a good life and this was what she had done? I felt so sorry for him. He'd been totally betrayed. All I could do at this stage was to offer him my support. It seemed tome his world was unravelling, and there was nothing I could do to help him with this. We needed to focus on the future, on our new lives together. Bill had a good job, he owned property, he clearly had access to other funds, and his earning potential was vast. We would be OK financially; I knew this. I just hoped Bill could deal with the revelations about Sofia and what she had done. I wanted to help in any way I could, so I resolved that I would do all I could to support him, love him, and help him to heal the wounds.

* * *

Life continued normally for another three months or so. I almost forgot about the German bank loan, as Bill just never mentioned it, and when I did, I always got the same 'It's taken care of' reply. I believed it would go away. I trusted him implicitly and believed him when he said it was being dealt with. Wedding preparations were in full swing when three months before the big day Bill once again came home ashen faced.

"You look like you've seen a ghost. What's happened?" I asked.

"I've been stupid, really, really stupid." He shook his head, tears in his eyes.

"Tell me," I said.

"When we had the company in Germany, I filtered off some money to put into an offshore account, it was on the Isle of Man; I've told you about it. There was about three hundred thousand pounds sterling. I've been bringing the money into

Switzerland bit by bit. I had fully intended to bring it all over by now, but when I met you, I got so distracted I didn't do it."

"OK, this is the money you've been subsidising your income from work with?"

"Yes, exactly," he said.

"I put it in an offshore account. To do this I set up a bogus company on the Isle of Man and appointed 'directors' of this company. These are just people you pay to put their name on the accounts. My name appears nowhere, as clearly it's a tax dodge, and I didn't want a paper trail to lead back to me."

"And you say Sofia knew about this?" I asked

"No, that was the whole point; I filtered the money away from the company because I wanted to keep something back for me. Anyway, I spoke to my contact at the bank over there today, and he told me the Government has frozen the account. I can no longer access it."

"Oh no, Bill, how much is in there?"

"Like I said, the best part of three hundred thousand pounds," at that time nearly three quarters of a million Swiss francs.

"But you can get it back, right? It's your money. Surely you just pay the tax on it, and they give it back?"

"No Sarah, it doesn't work like that. It's illegal money, and there is no paper trail to me, it's gone, I can't access it. I lost it all because I was so preoccupied with my relationship with you, that I didn't take care of it in time."

I felt terrible. It was my fault. He'd lost all his money.

"What shall we do?" I cried. "What about the wedding, can we still afford it? Shall we postpone it? I don't mind postponing it. We can cancel if you like and have a small wedding later on. I really wouldn't mind, I just want to give you a chance to recover from all this!"

"No, Sarah, no way. This is our big day and we'll go ahead as planned. It's taken care of anyway, don't worry about the money, it's only money after all! I can easily earn it back again. I'm just so angry with myself for taking my eye off the ball. First the loan Sofia took out, and now this. I could kick myself!"

"Oh Bill, I'm so sorry this is happening to you! But, what about the loan? Didn't you say you had a property in Germany? Can't you sell something to pay off the debt and start again?"

"I found out that the property in Germany is owned by Sofia's mother. Her mother hates me."

"What? So you mean she took out a loan in your name and used it to buy a house for her mother to live in? Whose name is on the deeds?"

"Her mother's; and it's a house with three apartments in, so she gets an income from it too."

"You have got to be kidding me! How can this be right? This is so unfair! You've been well and truly screwed over! I'm so sorry Bill!"

"Let's open a bottle of wine and I'll explain some things to you," he said.

So we sat and we talked; Bill opened up some more about his past. He told me that Sofia had been raised by her grandmother and had very little contact with her mother. He didn't speak kindly of Sofia's mother at all; there was clearly a lot of resentment there. Sofia had been the product of an extramarital affair, Bill told me. Her father was on a business trip when he met her mother and they embarked on the affair. Her father had a wife and children in Australia. When she found out she was pregnant, Sofia's mother refused any support from the father, and decided to bring up the baby by herself. She worked hard though, and as she was never around, the job of child rearing was left to her mother, Sofia's grandmother. Inevitably, the relationship between mother and daughter was strained, Bill said. Eventually they drifted apart, as Sofia got older. Bill explained that when he'd met Sofia, she'd had no contact at all with her mother for many years and was deeply resentful about her upbringing. It was Bill, said he, who finally persuaded her to re-establish contact with her mother and to track down her Australian relatives.

* * *

So, with Bill's help and encouragement, Sofia began to build bridges, and the relationship with her mother was slowly restored. She had also traced her Australian family, but sadly it was too late for her to meet her father, as he'd died some years before. She did manage to trace her half-brother and half-sisters though, and her relationship with her brother in particular was relatively good. Bill explained that he'd never 'connected' with Sofia's mother or German family at all. He said he'd always found the mother to be cold and hard- faced. He said it was a mutual dislike and often caused friction in the family. He said he was always 'an outsider' in Sofia's family, and felt he had never won the approval of her mother. He explained that her mother had appeared greedy, wanting to cash in wherever she could on Sofia, and as she could see Sofia had married a successful man, she wanted 'her share of the action'.

"She couldn't stand me," he said, "but it didn't stop her wanting to get whatever she could from me and Sofia."

When Sofia had died, and Bill had travelled to France, he told me he was acutely aware of her mother's feelings and had wanted to 'sort out the house' before she arrived on the scene. He described the scene once again, and how he'd struggled to clean up and get the dreadful stench of death from the air before her mother arrived. He explained how he'd wanted to protect her mother from the horror in the bedroom, and remove as much of Sofia's soiled belongings as possible. Burning the mattress was a priority, he'd said, as he couldn't bear the thought of her mother having to see where her daughter had lain. When Sofia's mother arrived, however, she was, according to Bill, apparently unmoved by the scene. She had headed straight for the living room, and started removing items from the house and loading them into her car.

"She ransacked the place," he said, shaking his head.

"She took books, CD's, porcelain, wedding gifts, anything and everything that wasn't pinned down."

He told of his incredulity, as she demanded repeatedly that he handover a pendant that she'd given to Sofia some years earlier.

"I don't have it!" he'd cried, but she insisted he find it. In the end he told me he threw Sofia's jewellery box at her.

"Here take it, take it all!" She'd searched the box, but couldn't find what she was looking for, and left. He then told me he'd found the pendant later that day, but had never handed it over to her, so angry was he at the way she'd behaved. He said that her family had all completely blanked him at the funeral. They'd blamed him for her death, because they knew he'd been seeking a divorce, which they believed was the reason she'd died.

"It wasn't the reason though," he explained. "I'm sure she was happy and in another relationship. When I first arrived on the scene there were two mugs on the coffee table, I think she had somebody with her that night. There was also a note, in her handwriting and addressed to a man called Ron. I only ever saw it once, and I didn't read it. The police took it away, and even though I asked to see it they refused. I just wonder if there was somebody else involved, but I guess we'll never know."

Since the funeral he'd had no more contact with Sofia's family. He explained that they had items in Germany which belonged to him, including a car, but they'd made no attempt to contact him, and he'd decided it would be best all-around to let it go completely.

For me, this would have been impossible. I am not the sort of person who can just 'let things go,' certainly not without a fight. If I felt people were wrongly accusing me, or suspecting me of something, I would just have to try and convince them they were wrong. That was clearly a huge difference between Bill's personality and mine. He seemed so 'resigned' to everything that had happened: from the loan, to the offshore money, to Sofia's family and their intense dislike of him. It was surely an unbearable strain on him, even if he did appear to be just shrugging it off. My head was spinning trying to digest what Bill had told me. I was starting to get a clearer picture about what had happened to Sofia and why she had taken her own life. I couldn't imagine how Bill must be feeling about all of this. Once again, I resolved to do all I could to help him put the past behind him, and give him a bright new future with me.

Chapter Five

The Start of Married Life

And so we arrived at the wedding day, and as I wrote in my journal, I was on cloud nine. I didn't think anything could possibly spoil things for us, despite all the 'rumblings' that were going on behind the scenes. Bill had an uncanny talent for reassuring me that everything would be OK. I trusted him completely. I took my lead from him, and as it appeared that he was relaxed, happy and confident, then so was I.

I can't describe the pride I felt at that time of my life. I was proud to be at Bill's side. I was full of admiration and respect for the man I loved, who had overcome so many knock backs to get to where he was today. I was filled with excitement and anticipation of our new life together, and the most exciting prospect of all, we were planning on starting a family right away. When I first met Bill, I was against the idea of children. I was so disillusioned with the opposite sex, and I lacked confidence in myself to the extent that I didn't think I could possibly make a good mother. I was also angry at the world in general. In my youthful naivety, I believed the world to be an unforgiving place, and I blamed many of my own problems on my perceived 'unlucky breaks'. I guess I could safely say I was pretty screwed up when I met Bill. He had changed all that by showing me such an overwhelming amount of love and attention that I really had come to believe

41

that I could achieve just about anything. He'd certainly helped me to get my confidence back up.

One evening, very early on in our relationship, I'd asked Bill about what he wanted for the future.

"I want you, and nothing else," he'd said.

"I want to take care of you, love you, give you the world. And I want us to have children together. We'd make the most beautiful children."

"You want more children?" I asked. "I'm surprised. I didn't think you'd want to do all that again."

"I do," he assured me. "I have so much love to give, and I'd be so honoured if you'd consider it."

And that was all the encouragement I'd needed. All of a sudden my attitude changed, and from that moment on, I'd been eagerly anticipating my life as a wife and mother. I wanted nothing more in the whole world.

* * *

The wedding was the fairytale I'd hoped it would be. I couldn't have asked for more: the setting, my friends and family, the dress, the venue. It was my day. Bill made it my day. He had invited his dad and stepmother, his three children, and a couple of other friends, but that was it. Most of the wedding party was made up of my friends and family. It was slightly awkward having his children there. I'd only met two of them before the day, and then only briefly. Their relationship with their father seemed somewhat strained. Outwardly they appeared to get on, but you couldn't miss the undercurrents, particularly on the wedding day. I wondered how it must have felt for them, seeing their father walk down the aisle again with a younger woman. There was only a five year age gap between Bill's oldest daughter and myself. They stayed for the ceremony, but left before the meal. Bill's family table, to the left of our top table, was almost empty. Despite this, however, it was a great day, and I couldn't have been happier.

The day after the wedding, we flew from Birmingham to Dubai for our honeymoon. The journey had been amazing. When the flight attendants had realised we were newlyweds, they had moved us into first class and plied us with wine for the entire duration of the journey. When we arrived, we were picked up at the airport in a Limousine, and whisked across Dubai to the Jumeirah Beach complex, and our waiting five star hotel.

When I saw our room I was almost in tears. I'd never been to a place so grand before. It was simply out of this world. Here I was, on my honeymoon, with so much to look forward to. Then, a very strange thing happened to me. I don't know if it was the alcohol, the emotion of the last few days, or just extreme tiredness, but as I walked onto the balcony and looked down at the lit swimming pool twelve storeys below, I experienced something I had never experienced before, and never want to again. A voice screamed at me from inside my head,

"This bubble will burst. This bubble will burst…GET OUT NOW!" And in that split second, I seriously considered throwing myself off the balcony. I don't honestly know what stopped me. The urge to do it was so overwhelming. It sends shivers down my spine to recall it. But I remember rit so clearly. It's a moment that I had nightmares about for years afterwards, and I still find it difficult to recall and explain. I had no reason whatsoever to feel suicidal. I had just married the man of my dreams; we were about to start a family. There was no logic at all to what I experienced in that moment. All I know is it was incredibly real, and the compulsion to end it all was absolutely all-consuming. I drew back from the balcony and sat down, shocked and confused. Bill then returned from ordering room service, and life went on as before.

* * *

After the dream honeymoon in Dubai, it was back to Switzerland and the start of our new life as a married couple. Baby making was on my mind. Moneymaking was on Bill's. Whilst on the honeymoon, we had discussed the debt left behind by Sofia and how to resolve the problem, given that Bill had unexpectedly found himself three hundred thousand quid worse off.

"If I continue to work for the company, the debt collecting authorities will seize my money at source," he'd explained.

"My only hope is to go back to consulting again," he'd said.

"We could set up a limited company and put you up as a company director. That way we declare a lower income for me, and the authorities won't be able to take anything away from us. It's a gamble, and it means we're starting from scratch, but as a consultant I can earn big bucks and we can make back the money I've lost."

"OK," I agreed, "That sounds like a good plan. You clearly have enough contacts that you won't be short of work, right?"

"Of course," he enthused. "I have contacts all over the place. At the very worst I might have to take the Japanese up on their offer, and we'd have to leave Switzerland for a couple of years. But I'd earn enough money in that time for us to retire on!"

He was so confident and self-assured. I felt safe. I just knew that despite the setback of losing his offshore money, and the legacy of debt left by Sofia, Bill would get things back on track. We'd be able to enjoy a peaceful and secure life.

"My dream," he'd said, "is to work only for another three to five years. After that I'd love to retire to the South of France, buy an old farm house and renovate it, and then open a small restaurant."

Cooking was his passion. He was a self-taught master chef. He could turn a cheese sandwich into gourmet cuisine. He was pretty much an expert at everything he did. This was one of the reasons I was so in awe of him. He could turn his hand to pretty much anything: from DIY to gardening, from engineering to design, from music to poetry. He was one of the brightest and most creative people I'd ever met. No, he was THE most creative and intelligent person I'd ever met. There didn't seem to be a subject about which he didn't have vast knowledge. I used to joke and call him a walking encyclopaedia. He loved to throw dinner parties. He'd impress our guests with the finest wines, and the most breath taking cuisine (he'd spend nine or ten hours in the kitchen preparing the food from scratch), and then he'd literally hold court around the dining table, impressing his knowledge upon us all. He would argue his point until he'd won any debate, on any subject. Sometime she would keep guests up well into the early hours, just to ensure his point had been made. He had the gift of the gab, for sure. And it was because of this that I had no hesitation in backing his decision to hand in his notice at our company and set up his own one-man consultancy business. I was convinced he couldn't go wrong.

* * *

During the two years I'd known Bill, he had been forging a strong working relationship with some clients of the company we worked for. It was these clients he'd been entertaining the night before he met me, and why he'd been late into work that day. The clients were government officials from an Eastern European country, who were potentially interested in awarding a huge contract to our company for military supplies. Governments spend big bucks on defence, but they move slowly, so our company had been cultivating the relationship over an extended period. Bill was an integral part of the team. He'd aligned himself well between the clients and the company. So much so, that when he informed the company of his decision to go independent as a consultant, they immediately agreed to use his services to continue to liaise with the clients, until such a time as the project was finalised. This was a great starting place for the new business venture. Bill was relieved to be able to leave fixed employment, yet continue his working relationship with the company, and reap the rewards of being independent once more. When I asked him about the German bank debt, he reassured me that this was now 'all taken care of' and that we had nothing left to fear.

Bill left work at the end of August. A new chapter was about to begin for us. In September I fell pregnant with our first child. Life could not have been better. From the moment I fell pregnant it was clear to both of us that I would leave work in order to raise our child. Bill was to be the bread winner. He was already in the process of contacting old business partners to let them know he was back on the market. Before long the contracts would be flooding in, he said. We decided he needed to set up an office in our apartment in order to run his business effectively and professionally. We'd acquired an extra room from our landlord, and Bill had decided to convert half into a walk-in wardrobe, and use the other half as his office. He spent a great deal of time doing this. He designed and built the wardrobe from scratch, and he spent a small fortune fitting out his office space. He seemed to spend very little time actually 'working', but as the company had agreed to a monthly rate, our finances remained fluid. I'd often wondered when he ever fitted in any work whilst he was actually employed by the company. He always seemed to spend more time emailing me, or researching various things on the web, than actually completing his paid work. Nobody ever seemed to complain about this though, so I assumed it was because he was just so talented and good at what he did, he could complete his tasks in half the time of any 'normal' person. Nothing changed once he began working from home. I assumed he was achieving vast amounts of work, even though he appeared to spend all his time on non-work related activities. I handed in my notice at work, and began to focus solely on the pregnancy, reassured that Bill would take care of everything else.

* * *

In October, Bill once again whisked me off to the same luxury hotel on Lake Geneva. We spent another glorious weekend being pampered, no expense spared. My bump was starting to show now, and I was really feeling as though I was blooming. Once again Bill enjoyed drawing attention to me when we were out, constantly patting my stomach and letting people know how proud he was of me. I honestly felt truly blessed. As the New Year came around, the pregnancy was progressing well. Bill was busy working with the Eastern European clients. He'd intimated tome that he might have a possibility to work for them directly as well, again as a consultant. This was an exciting prospect, as he'd already made it clear he would be charging a phenomenal fee for his services. As I understood it, he was to orchestrate the 'deal' between our company in Switzerland and the clients, and once it was complete, he would then act as the interface between the client and our company to oversee the contract through to delivery and beyond. I had asked him if he was actually allowed to do this, as I was sure there was a clause in his consultancy contract with the Swiss company, which precluded him for leaving and immediately working with a customer. But he assured me that both parties had agreed to it, as he was the person in the best position to oversee the logistic and commercial strategies from both sides of the fence. I was pretty much engrossed with the pregnancy at this time, and not paying so much attention to what Bill was doing work wise. I was only really interested in home making and all things baby related. I do recall, however, some rather clandestine activity to do with the European clients around this time.

"They've asked me to provide them with some information, but I can't allow it to be traced back to me."

"What sort of information? Are you sure you want to be getting involved with that? Hadn't you better ask somebody here first?"

"Sarah, don't worry, I know what I'm doing. I don't need to ask people's permission like some schoolboy. I'm providing them with pricing information that is in the public domain anyway, so I'm not breaking any rules. I'm simply assisting them and scoring some brownie points with them at the same time. This is about our future after all, and they want to employ me, so I want to impress them."

"But are you sure this won't upset our company? They're the ones who are paying you right now, after all?"

"Sarah, I wish I'd never mentioned this to you now. Just relax and concentrate on the baby." And so that's what I did. I remember a package being couriered, no return address. I think it contained a CD, but I can't be sure.

Then, about a month before the baby was due, I was off work with a nasty bout of bronchitis. Bill was looking after me, and as usual was spending very little time in the office. One afternoon, the phone rang; it was his ex-boss from the company, the man in charge of his consultancy contract. Bill hung up the phone and came into the bedroom ashen faced. I knew this look by now.

"What's happened?"

"He's cancelled my contract, the arsehole!"

"What? Why? Can he do that?"

"I don't know why. The guy's a tit; he's just got a personal problem with me. He made up some cock and bull reason about not having resources anymore." He was shaking with anger.

"You need to go to his boss, sort it out! They can't just let you go; you're in the middle of a big contract!"

"They can, they can terminate my contract at any time. This has nothing to do with my work or me, Sarah; I'm an invaluable asset to them and they know it. This is some jumped up arsehole who feels threatened by me; it's purely personal. Don't worry; I'll sort it. I'll speak to the clients, and I'll get them to take me on. It'll be fine. I'm just angry with them for doing this to us now. You don't need this stress in your condition."

He was damn right I didn't. He'd barely been working as a consultant more than a few months, I was about to leave work and give birth, and he'd just lost his only source of income. To top it all, he'd just gone and ordered a lease car via the new company he'd set up (of which I was joint director). It was a brand new four-by-four. He'd decided we needed it for our expanding family. He'd taken great pleasure in ordering all the added extras that come with these vehicles, and I felt he was every bit as excited about its arrival as he was about the impending birth of our first child. I tried to tell myself to relax, to do as Bill said and not worry too much. He'd fix it; he was more than capable. And if he couldn't resolve the issue with the company, he'd just go and work for somebody else. It would be OK. Bill knew what he was doing. I was sure we'd be fine.

Chapter Six

A Child is Born, and More...

For our first wedding anniversary, Bill took me to an alpine hotel. We dined on the terrace overlooking the lake; it was a glorious Sunday lunchtime. He'd organised for the table to be decorated with lilies, and as usual no expense was spared, this despite the fact that I'd just left work (on four months maternity leave) and we had no income. I tried my best to ignore the niggling worries in the back of my mind, and focus only on Bill and the baby. Two days later she was born. My waters had broken in the middle of the night, and eight hours later she was with us. Lucy was our first born. It was the most emotional moment of my life when I first laid eyes on her. It had been a difficult labour and birth, and had ended up with lots of doctors running around attending to my injuries. I'd lost a lot of blood and was very weak, but it all paled into insignificance once I held her in my arms. Everything else just dissolved away, and there was only Lucy, Bill and myself in the world. I marvelled at the little miracle in my arms. She was perfect in every way. Once back on the ward I telephoned my mum. I had to speak to her.

"Mum," I said "I know now how much you love me," and I did. Not until you hold your own child in your arms can you appreciate the love a parent feels for their offspring. It's like nothing else on earth. It's indescribable.

After five days in hospital it was time to return home. Not only was I eager to get out of the hospital and begin looking after Lucy by myself, I was also very aware that Bill needed to return to work. It had been almost two months now since his contract was cancelled and still there was nothing on the horizon from the Eastern European country he'd been so convinced were going to take him on. My parents arrived in Switzerland the day I came out of hospital. I wasn't really strong enough to cope at that point. Physically I'd taken a huge knock with the birth, and I was really grateful to have my mum about for support. Whilst Lucy had been quiet and easy to manage in the hospital, as soon as we brought her home that all changed. She screamed uncontrollably from mid-afternoon until late in the evening. As a new mum I was feeling extremely delicate and unsure of myself. Every time she started screaming, Bill would take her off me and try to comfort her. He seemed so confident with what he was doing, at the time I thought he really did know best.

"I've had children before Sarah, you haven't. Leave her to me. I'll bring her to you when she needs feeding."

I was struggling with breast-feeding. I was in excruciating pain, and I was feeling very sorry for myself. Lucy was feeding constantly through the night, and between that and Bill's snoring, I got no rest at all. It was like wading through treacle. I started to feel quite hopeless. Lucy was clearly suffering with colic, and I felt it was somehow my fault. Bill's nerves were fraught too. He adored Lucy and was reluctant to let her out of his sight. Even when I was with her he was constantly there. I felt he was watching what I was doing; I felt so unsure of myself I tended to allow him to take over. He was the one who'd had practice at this, after all.

When Lucy was three weeks old, Bill went on a business trip to 'clinch' his future contract with the Easter European clients. We were now living on my maternity pay, and with a new baby things were going to be tight. There was a lot riding on this trip, and even though we couldn't really afford for him to be making a trip right now, I knew we had no choice.

I was horrified when Bill rang me on his arrival and announced that the hotel he'd booked into was full, and the only room they had available was the Presidential Suite.

"Can't you book into another hotel?" I asked, incredulously.

"Sadly not, dear," he'd said. "There's a huge conference on and all the hotels in the city are fully booked. Looks like I'll just have to stay here and pay the money."

I was really upset. We certainly couldn't afford for Bill to be staying in exclusive Presidential Suites right now. Thank God he was so confident of getting the contract; we were going to need it after this. But it wasn't to be. After a week of entertaining 'clients' at his Presidential Suite, and wining and dining them of an evening in the best restaurants in town, Bill came back without a contract.

"It will happen," he assured me. "My contacts are just ironing out the details and getting the financial side of things cleared. "In the meantime, I've got several other things in the pipeline, so don't worry, it'll be fine." But it wasn't fine; in fact it was anything but. After that trip, Bill was never invited to visit the clients again.

When Lucy was about eight weeks old, Bill got a call one morning from one of his ex-colleagues in the company where we'd both worked. Once again, I saw that ashen face.

"You're not going to believe this," he sighed. "Apparently an email has been circulated within the company warning employees that they are not to have any further contact with me, and most certainly are not to talk to me about any company business. They are saying that they're going to bring a criminal suit against me."

"They're going to do what?" I thought I was going to faint.

"They're accusing me of breaching a contract or something. I'm not sure." Just then, the doorbell rang. It was the postman, bringing registered post. It was a letter from the Company Lawyer, accusing Bill of 'stealing company secrets' and selling them to a third party. This was, according to the company, in direct contravention of the Data Protection Act he'd signed when they employed him.

"This is bollocks!" he said. "I've done nothing wrong. This is just my idiot boss trying to get back at me because he has some sort of personal vendetta. They don't have any evidence anyway. They're bluffing."

"Are you really sure?" I had to ask this question, as I was remembering all the cloak and dagger sending of the CD a few months earlier.

"What about that CD you sent? It has to be about that, right? What was on it? Was it confidential information?"

"No, it bloody well wasn't!" He raised his voice to me for the very first time. "I told you at the time, that was information which was already in the public domain; the clients could have accessed it themselves if they'd wanted to. I was just doing them a favour. I didn't do anything wrong."

"What are we going to do now?" I was completely horrified. I felt so angry that Bill's former boss would turn on him this way and try to wreck his new business, when I'd just given birth to our first child. The more I thought about it, the sicker I felt. This simply could not be happening! "We need to get a lawyer," he said. "Leave it with me."

* * *

And so I left it with him. There wasn't much else I could do. This was supposed to be the happiest time of my life. I was a brand new mother. Now, at two months in, I was finally starting to find my feet and gain a bit of confidence with Lucy. I'd been looking forward to joining the ranks of the stay at home mummy. Previously I'd been working all the time, but now I had Lucy, there was a whole new world of ex-pat wives to discover. The only problem was that most of the ex-pat wives and mothers were connected to the company, and the company had issued a remit to its employees not to have anything to do with us.

I received a flood of phone calls and visits, mostly from people just wanting to hear our side of the story. I told them what I knew, which wasn't a great deal. I could feel the waves of disapproval, and slowly but surely, apart from a select few, people started to distance themselves from us. This was such a disappointment for me. I was enraged, but equally I was bitterly disappointed and hurt. I hated being the butt of people's gossip. To me, it felt like my world had collapsed.

We saw a solicitor and he informed us that although the company had threatened legal action, he very much doubted they were in a position to take it, as it seemed the accusations were based purely on circumstantial evidence. This supported Bill's theory that he was the victim of a personal vendetta. Surely, if there really were grounds for criminal proceeding, the company would take action? The fact it wasn't going to did seem to vindicate Bill. I strived to remain as supportive as I could. I stood up for Bill, went to the solicitor's meetings with him, and tried to remain defiant about the injustice of it all. We spent hours picking over it and analysing what had gone wrong between Bill, the company and the clients. Bill constantly reassured me that he was in no way to blame for it all. He'd simply tried to help, and his ex-boss had got jealous of his new position, and decided to try to wreck his chances with that client. I was devastated that Bill's ex-boss could be so cruel. I'd always though the and Bill had had a good working relationship, and couldn't understand how a man could set out to try to ruin another man's career, especially when she knew that his wife had just recently given birth.

"But I want people to know you're innocent! The way it's been left makes it seem like you've done wrong. People think I'm involved as well. They think I somehow helped you to steal company secrets. What if I need to go back to work? I'll never get my job back there now!"

"Sarah, darling, please! There are some battles that are worth fighting and there are others that are best left alone. The people who really count have stuck by us. Who cares what other people think? It doesn't matter to me what people say. You don't need your job back there anyway. People who think you're involved are all narrow-minded losers. You don't need them. You only need me. As long as we've got each other, and as long as you trust me, things will be OK. I love you, and I promise to sort this out, OK?"

It had to be OK, because I didn't have any choice. Once again I was frustrated by Bill's 'couldn't care less what people think' attitude. I cared very much what people thought. I wanted him to clear his name, not just let it drop. There was no changing it though. After many legal meetings and letters back and forth, our lawyer persuaded them to drop the action and let it go. The company reluctantly gave Bill a very basic reference, on the condition that he stayed away from any of its clients, and he never set foot on company ground again. So now here we were, with fewer friends, Bill with no business credibility in Switzerland, no income, and lawyer's fees to pay. It was quite a scary place to be, and I was starting to feel the pressure. Despite all the supposed business possibilities Bill had enthused about a month or two earlier, not one new contract was forthcoming. I was starting to panic.

"It's OK, Sarah," he'd reassured me. "I'll just go contracting again. I can walk into a contracting job no problem; they're ten a penny. I'll do what I have to do for you and Lucy."

It was another month before he finally found a contracting job. It was for a large UK company, and it meant he had to commute. The job was, in Bill's words 'menial and completely beneath me' but he'd had to take it on as there simply was no other income, and we had bills to pay. He reluctantly took it, and we decided to head to the UK for a five week stretch to enable me to get away from all the recent controversy in Switzerland. Bill took digs from Monday to Friday, and travelled back to see us at the weekends. He hated being away from us, and he hated his new job. I was happy to know we at least had an income again, but did feel sad that we couldn't be together as a family. Still, the time Bill was away gave me a chance to bond with Lucy for the first time. I'd really struggled with feeding her since birth. It was something I'd always wanted to do, and I'd assumed it would come naturally. I wasn't prepared for how difficult and painful it would be for me. I realised I had many inhibitions, and I just couldn't relax with feeding in public. It was difficult to get into a routine, and I was always so conscious of Lucy crying for food whilst we were out and me not being able to feed her. I tried to time all of my activities around feeding times, so we wouldn't be out when she needed to nurse. It meant I was restricted, and I felt inadequate. Bill often commented on this problem. He found it frustrating that I was so stressed about it, and that it restricted our social life. When Lucy was about three months, some friends of mine had come to visit us from abroad. They too had a little girl the same age as Lucy, and my friend was breast-feeding successfully. One day during their visit we'd taken a cable car trip up the mountain, and had stopped for refreshments at a busy restaurant. We'd sat at a table away from the main crowd, but as it was busy we weren't far from the bustle. Both babies had cried for food at the same time. My friend had immediately started to discreetly feed her little girl. Lucy kept crying, and I was trying to pacify her by rocking and cuddling her. I didn't want to feed her here.

"She needs feeding," Bill had said.

"I know!" I reluctantly started to try and position her, but I was tense and fumbling around with my clothes. I felt clumsy and stupid. I felt everybody was looking at me.

"Have you got a problem feeding her in public?" Bill said, smiling at me. He knew I had a problem with it!

"I can't do it here," I said, almost in tears by now. "I'll have to go somewhere more private. Can you come with us please?"

"Why don't you go to the toilets?" he said.

"I don't want to feed her in the toilets. Please will you come with me?" Bill sighed and stood up. He wasn't happy about leaving his beer and his conversation with my friend's husband. We left the restaurant and looked for somewhere that I could feed. I was beside myself, as Lucy was very distressed by now. I couldn't find anywhere to sit, and eventually ended up sitting on a rock next to the hiking pathway. I began to feed Lucy.

"Jesus!" exclaimed Bill. "This is bloody ridiculous; you may as well have sat in there! It's no more private here that it is in the restaurant!"

I burst into tears. He really didn't understand how it felt for me. I felt like a loser, and I'd really hoped for more support. As soon as she was fed, he took her from me, and held her until it was time to return home. It wasn't until we were back in the UK that I realised how much the feeding was affecting me and my bonding with Lucy.

Once Lucy hit the sixteen-week stage, I weaned her onto a bottle, and it was like a fog had lifted from my life. This, coupled with the fact that I was relaxed, at home with my parents, and that I had much more one on one time with Lucy now Bill was working again, meant we suddenly bonded, and I was overjoyed to have my little girl to myself for the very first time.

* * *

By the time we returned to Switzerland, my maternity pay
had stopped, and I was now officially unemployed. Because
I'd left the company, my pension fund was paid out to me in
a lump sum. It wasn't much I suppose, maybe in the region
of thirty thousand Swiss francs, but it was the money I'd
worked for, and it was supposed to be for our future. Sadly,
we were so hard up by that time that the money was absorbed
into the household costs. Lawyer's fees were paid, the credit
card bills were paid (from the luxury trip which resulted in
no contract), and the backlog of invoices that had built up
during the time when Bill wasn't earning. It was all gone. I
tried not to let this bother me too much. Bill was working
again now after all, and as he was so confident about earning
it all back, I carried on believing that was what would
happen.

Within a week of starting the UK contract, Bill was coming
home telling me how they wanted to keep him on long term,
and pay him more money, give him more responsibility etc.
Within three weeks, he was coming home telling me what an
arsehole his new boss was. Inevitably, Bill's new boss was
quite a bit younger than him (as was his last one) and in
Bill's eyes, he was perceived to be a jumped up jerk (as was
his last boss). It wasn't long before there was considerable
friction between Bill and his new boss, and as a result of this,
it looked as though he might not have his contract extended
after all.

Not long after returning to Switzerland, rescue came in the
form of a phone call from Bill's friend in France. He worked

as an HR president for a large company in the South of France, and knowing our predicament, he'd managed to line Bill up for a consultancy job with them. It was the break we really needed. The money was much more in line with what Bill was worth, and he could start immediately. It was also a long-term contract. Clearly he had no choice but to take it. There was no way he was going to get work in Switzerland after what had happened with the company, and France was the place Bill had always wanted to return to. It seemed that this was just meant to be.

I was adapting to life on my own with Lucy. Of course I missed Bill like mad during the week, but in many ways I was glad to get some freedom and routine back. I was gaining confidence as a mother, and my relationship with Lucy was blooming. I was starting to make new friends, people who weren't connected to the company and didn't know about recent events. I really felt that there was reason to be positive again, after the rocky few months we'd had.

Then came the next bombshell. I'd been feeling unwell for many weeks. I put it down to stress and the rapid weight loss I'd experienced in the last few months. It was also the time of year for flu. I'd enrolled Lucy in an aqua baby course, and during her very first swimming lesson. I had this overwhelming sensation. I can't really describe it, but it was as though I suddenly became aware of my stomach whilst in the water. It felt.....different. On the way home, I impulsively drove past a chemist and stopped to pick up a pregnancy test. I didn't believe for a second there was a chance I was pregnant. Since all the problems had started, and since the birth of Lucy, Bill and I had barely been near one another, but I needed to rule it out. I did the test as soon as I got home, and immediately wished I hadn't. It was positive.

Chapter Seven

The Cracks Begin to Appear

My world seemed to grind to a halt. This was certainly not what I was expecting or planning. I'd only just got to grips with being Lucy's mum, and now there was another baby on the way. Not only that, but I was living here alone for most of the time. How on earth was I going to cope? Bill called at that moment. He was sitting in the departure lounge of the airport about to fly back to Switzerland for the weekend. He immediately picked up from my voice that something was up.

"What's happened?" he asked.

"Nothing," I answered. "I'll tell you when you get home."

"No, tell me now. I can hear it in your voice, something's up. What is it?"

"I've had a shock. I really need to tell you face to face though."

"Is it what I think it is?" he asked. "Are you pregnant?"

"How did you guess??"

"Just a hunch!"

"What are we going to do?" I cried. "I'm not ready for this. Lucy is barely six months old!"

"Do you want to know what I think?"

"OK"

"I think it's fantastic news!"

"You do?" I was genuinely shocked. It's not as though we were in a very financially stable situation, and with everything that had gone on these past few months, I was amazed that Bill could react so calmly to the news that we were about to bring another child into the world. But he was over the moon, and when he came home that night he swept me up in his arms and held me tight. He made me feel secure again, and I felt that everything would be OK, whatever life threw at us.

When I went to the Doctor's I was shocked to discover that I was already in the tenth week of the pregnancy. I was going through such mixed emotions. I really wasn't sure how I was going to cope. I was worried I wouldn't be able to give enough attention to another child; Lucy needed me! Bill was very reassuring.

"Children are easy peasy," he'd said. "You'll be just fine. It's not rocket science." And of course I knew he was right; raising children was not rocket science. Even I could manage it.

* * *

When Bill started work in France, life improved dramatically. He'd managed to negotiate a four-day week, which meant he was home from Thursday night until Sunday afternoon. He took digs close to the office and was much happier to be back in France than he had been whilst he was in the UK. He even seemed to get on OK with his boss this time. Things seemed to be settling down for us. I was happy with my circle of friends; the rumours and gossip appeared to have died down, and I really thought we were moving on from the dramas.

Then, in late November, I answered a knock at the door to be greeted with a registered delivery. It was a court order for the German bank loan. I called Bill in France

"I thought this was taken care of? I suppose it was too much to expect that they'd go away. It's a hell of a lot of money after all. What on earth are we going to do?"

"I'll get hold of the solicitor and see if we can negotiate a repayment plan," Bill reassured me. But the bank weren't interested in negotiating anything; they wanted their money. They seemed to believe Bill had the means to pay them back the full amount, and they weren't prepared to settle for anything less. In early December, they froze Bill's bank accounts. He quickly organised for his wages to be transferred into my bank account and changed the company papers to make it look as though I was the chief bread winner, and he was earning only a relatively small amount. This meant that from now on, everything would be in my name: the car, the bank accounts, and the company. Bill had many meetings with the Swiss authorities, who were pursuing the claim on behalf of the Germans, but they were relentless, they kept pushing. It was an incredibly stressful time, and for me it was worse because Bill didn't want me to talk to anybody about it. I spoke only to my mum about the stress we were dealing with. I questioned Bill once again about the loan and what he knew about it. He once again told me that he'd not known anything about it; that Sofia had done this behind his back and there was nothing he could do. There were no extenuating circumstances because she was now deceased. The loan had his name on it, and therefore it fell to him to sort it out. I was in turmoil again.

How could Sofia have done this? Why would a wife steal money from her own husband? And moreover, why on earth had she not tried to talk to him about this? He was a reasonable man after all, and their separation had been amicable. Surely they could have sorted out a repayment plan. The money was used to buy a house for her mother; they could have re-mortgaged it. No amount of money is worth losing your life over. I felt sad for Sofia, but equally I felt frustrated that she'd left such a mess behind her, and now Bill and I were being punished for her mistakes. It all seemed so unfair.

"What about the house in France?" I asked him.

"They don't know about that, and we're not going to tell them!" He'd replied. "They would seize it if they knew, and it's all we've got left!"

"Well, shouldn't we transfer the ownership of that house into my name as well? Just in case?"

"Yes, we'll have to. You'll have to come to France so we can organise it. In the meantime, don't mention it!"

* * *

In December that year, Bill told me he was going to declare himself bankrupt. As part of the procedure, a notice would be published in the local paper, to allow any other creditors a chance to come forward to stake their claim. The stress was almost too much for me. We'd only just started to recover from the accusations of insider dealing, and now Bill's name was going to be published in the paper as part of a bankruptcy process. I cried for a week. Once I knew about the notice in the paper, I felt compelled to start telling people, to get Bill's side of the story in first, and let people know he was just a victim, that his second wife had cheated him. As usual, Bill seemed less affected by it all than I was. He just wasn't at all bothered by what people thought of him.

"I know I've done nothing wrong," he'd said. "I don't need to explain myself to anybody. I couldn't give a toss what people think of me."

But I gave a toss. I cared a great deal. I wanted to shout out from the rooftops that this was not Bill's fault, that he was the victim in this. I wanted them to understand that his second wife had screwed him over for money and left him with this debt. I wanted to defend my husband. I wanted everybody to see that this wasn't his fault.

Inevitably though, the whispers started again. People were kind and sympathetic to my face, but I knew that as soon as my back was turned the gossip was flowing. Switzerland had been my dream; my life there was everything I'd ever wanted. I wanted to bring my children up in this wonderful country. I loved the place and the people, yet it was all turning sour. I felt uncomfortable wherever I went, like people were pointing the finger. All I'd wanted was a quiet life, yet it seemed controversy followed Bill wherever he went. My Swiss dream was turning into a nightmare.

* * *

The day the bailiffs came to the house was one of the worst for me. Here I was, six months pregnant and holding my nine-month-old baby, whilst three men came and sorted through all our belongings. Bill managed to smooth talk them though, the way he managed to smooth talk most people. "Everything you see belongs to my wife" He'd explained. From the Bang and Olufsen stereo to the furniture, the four-by-four on the driveway; I brought it all into the marriage, apparently.

And he got away with it. I don't know how, but he got away with it. They left with nothing, and not long after the process was frozen, as the Bank in Germany didn't come up with the money to actually force the bankruptcy through. Nevertheless, it was becoming abundantly clear that life in Switzerland was never going to be the same. After the threats of legal action for insider dealing, and now a bankruptcy proceeding, it was clear Bill would not be able to get work there again. We took the decision to leave and move to France as soon as the baby was safely in the world.

* * *

One day early in the New Year, Bill came home and excitedly told me that he had the chance to work as a broker for a deal between an Arabian airline and an aircraft manufacturer. He enthused that through his 'contacts,' he'd established this relationship, and was sure he could broker the deal and take a ten percent cut, netting us a profit of well over a million dollars.

This was an exciting prospect! It would potentially solve all our problems in one fell swoop. Bill was enthusiastic about the deal, telling our friends at every opportunity he got, how we were about to become overnight millionaires. In the meantime, I'd booked a trip to France. I wanted so much to get away from Switzerland and the constant reminders of recent months. I wanted nothing more than for our family to be together again. Switzerland had gone sour for me now, and I wasn't coping well with all the recent stresses and strains. I asked Bill to organise for us to see a Notaire whilst in France so we could transfer ownership of the house there. I was acutely aware that this was the only bit of collateral we had left, and as there was no guarantee the German bank was gone for good, I was keen to secure the property for Bill's parents. Bill seemed a bit reluctant at first, and I wasn't really sure why. But eventually he made the appointment and we drove to rural France to complete the paperwork.

It turned out it wasn't to be straightforward though. The house wasn't just in Bill's name. He bought it in both his and Sofia's names, but before they were married, so it was in Sofia's maiden name. The Notaire explained that, under French inheritance law, her next of kin would inherit Sofia's share of house. Fifty percent of her share would go to her mother, and the rest would be divided equally between any siblings she had. This was of course another blow. Bill was furious.

"I bought that house with my hard earned money!" He explained. "I even paid for it in cash!"

"Why did you put it in joint names then? You weren't married at the time, and you paid for it. So why did you put it in her name?"

"I don't know; it was a gesture of goodwill I suppose. I wanted to show her I trusted her." This was a strange thing to say. Bill had told me that he and Sofia were no more than just good friends, and that the marriage was purely one of convenience. I found it odd that Bill would buy a house with her and pay for it with cash, just as a 'gesture of goodwill.' I put it down to his unfailing generosity.

* * *

"There is one thing we can do," said the Notaire.

"We can put the house into your wife's name, if you give me a written statement that you have tried to contact the relatives of your late wife, and that her mother is in fact deceased."

"Well, she probably is dead by now," Bill had fumed. "I'm not letting that old bag get her hands on any more of my money. It's bad enough she's living in a house paid for by me, and they have one of my cars, they're not getting their hands on this as well."

"Very well," said the Notaire, "I'll draw up the papers, but it will cost you something in the region of ten thousand Euros."

"Ten thousand!" I'd exclaimed. We didn't have a spare ten thousand Euros; things were still really tight after running up debts whilst Bill hadn't been working. There was no way we could afford that right now. Another blow.

"Not to worry," Bill had said. "It's probably best if we sit on it for a while anyway; maybe the old woman really will die in the meantime. The house is secure for the time being, we don't need to worry about the German banks right now. Let's let the dust settle". I agreed with Bill. I wasn't happy about doing something illegal anyway. We'd had enough problems in the last twelve months; the last thing we needed would be any more threats of legal action. Maybe once Bill had sold these aircraft we could sort it all out then .I spent the rest of the time in France driving around looking at potential places to live once the baby was born. I was trying to work up some enthusiasm for the place, but to me it seemed so run down and unappealing after living in pristine Switzerland for so long. Still, I kept telling myself all that mattered was that our family could finally be together. I felt like our lives had been on hold for so long now, and I was just waiting to be able to finally enjoy family life as it was meant to me, instead of all this stress and hassle, and being on my own most of the time. On the Sunday before we were due to return to Switzerland, we'd eaten at a local restaurant. As we were leaving the restaurant I experienced a huge contraction. It took my breath away. I was twenty three weeks pregnant at the time. As we drove back to Bill's digs, the contractions continued but less painful. They were coming regularly.

"Shall I phone an ambulance?" Bill was frantic.

"No, please. I don't want any more stress. If we phone an ambulance I will panic and that won't help. I just need to sit quietly and hope it passes. Please look after Lucy for me."

Eventually the contractions became less regular and less painful, but it was a warning of things to come. We travelled back to Switzerland and I resumed life as a single mum, trying to look to the future and be happy about the move to France and hopefully a clean slate when we got there. Bill had been hopeful that his contract was going to last for at least another twelve months, and was extremely confident that his services would be required way into the future.

"The company is in a mess," he'd say. "The right arm doesn't know that the left is doing. They need my expertise to sort them out. I'll have work for the next ten years!" It was a pity that Bill had yet another awful boss in this post. Their relationship had started off well, but as Bill was so much older and infinitely better qualified than his boss, this once again led to friction.

"He's trying to make life difficult for me," he'd say. "He's a jumped up twerp who hasn't got a clue what he's doing. He doesn't have the capacity to understand my way of thinking. I have to try to use simple language when I talk to him. Basically I'm far too big for his department, and he feels threatened by me."

 Not again, it seemed all Bill's bosses felt threatened by Bill's superiority. I guess when you're that clever you must come up against this all the time. I just wished he could get on with his bosses; they were the ones responsible for our bread and butter after all. I wished Bill would rein it in a bit, and see that we needed his boss more than his boss needed Bill. I bit my tongue though; I had other things to concentrate on.

One morning in early March, I'd woken up with strong contractions once again. I tried breathing through them, but they didn't abate. Trying to keep calm, I got Lucy up and dressed, then called the Doctor. Before I knew it I was in the Doctors surgery hooked up to a machine. The contractions were registering at regular intervals, but they weren't powerful enough to put me into full labour.

"This is a warning," the Doctor had said. "You really need to slowdown or this baby will come too early. Your body hasn't really recovered from the first birth, and you've been overdoing it. You need to get help now, and you need to get rest wherever you can. You need to stay off your feet or I'm going to have to put you into hospital. We can't allow the baby to come yet."

How was I supposed to stay off my feet? I was living alone with my ten-month-old baby for most of the week! Fortunately for me help was at hand. As soon as I told my friends what was going on they all rallied around. One of my good friends organised in home help for me, to be paid for by our health insurance, and between them, they organised shifts to come and help out with shopping and taking care of Lucy. Bill was frustrated that he couldn't help, but I assured him there was nothing he could do, and that we were in good hands. I just needed to take it as easy as possible, and avoid stress, as the contractions were still coming almost every time I stood up. But avoiding stress didn't seem possible. One Monday morning when I was about twenty-nine weeks pregnant, I answered the door to yet another court order addressed to Bill. This time the demand for money was from GE Capital Bank, in Switzerland. The amount being demanded was twenty five thousand Swiss francs. There must have been some mistake. What on earth was this? I was shaking as I walked slowly down the stairs and into Bill's office to call him. Lucy was sitting at my feet playing with her toys. I got Bill on the phone.

"It's me," I said. "I'm sitting down, and I'm trying to be calm; I'm shaking a bit but I'm not having contractions."

'What's happened?' he almost whispered.

"There's a court order here with your name on it. It's from a Swiss Bank, for twenty five thousand. It's a mistake, right?" There was a pause.

"No, it's not a mistake. That was the wedding."

Chapter Eight

A Problem Pregnancy

I couldn't get annoyed with him over the phone. For some
reason, I didn't feel I had a right to. It had been 'my' day
after all. Even though I had never pushed for any of the
grandiose extras, he had done it all because he thought it was
what I had wanted. I sat there for a good ten minutes, trying
to digest it. Trying to recall the conversation we'd had when
he told me he'd lost all his money. I clearly remembered
telling him we'd postpone the wedding. I also remembered
clearly acknowledging that there was no way we should be so
extravagant, having just lost such a fortune. I would have
happily made cutbacks; I certainly wouldn't have wanted to
run up a debt, just to have a fancy wedding. And that was the
next thing. Why hadn't he told me he was going to borrow
the money? Because he knew I'd try to stop him? Moreover,
why had he taken another loan, despite knowing he had a
massive debt from Germany running in his name? When did
he default on this loan? It must have been months of arrears
according to the court order in front of me. He'd not paid a
single instalment in months. Surely they'd sent reminders?
No bank would just issue a court order like that without
sending several reminders and demands. Why the hell had
Bill not mentioned this to me? He'd lied to me! We were
supposed to be a team, a partnership, yet he'd kept this from
me. Why? To protect me? All these questions, and I simply

78

didn't have any answers. I felt guilty. He'd done this to give me the wedding I'd dreamed of. He'd kept it from me because he knew I'd worry. I just really wished he'd talked to me. Finding out like this, on top of everything else that was happening with the pregnancy, was just adding insult to injury.

When Bill came home that weekend I tried to talk to him about the bank loan, but he was dismissive.

"Look, when I took that loan I had no way of knowing what was going to happen with work," he said.

"Well, exactly," I replied. "You took it not knowing if you were even going to have a job in a few months' time."

"No, you've got it wrong," he replied. "I took it because I thought that within a few months I'd have my Isle of Man money back, and I intended to pay for it all in one go, before the interest racked up."

"Oh, so you took the loan out before you knew you'd lost the money, not after?" I was confused. Was this the money he'd been subsidising his income with?

"Yes, now can we leave this, please? I've got enough to worry about, you know. It's bad enough I don't get to see my daughter every day, and you're here, having to fend for yourself on bed rest, people coming into our home and taking over the running of it, and I'm not here to help you. I've also got problems with my boss. He's turned into a complete arsehole. He won't listen to my recommendations, and I think he's trying to undermine my position in the department. He's practically threatening me with not extending my contract if I don't toe the line. The little jumped up prick. I can barely bring myself to work with a person like that.

Oh great. Another arsehole boss who was making life difficult. Here we were, no money in the bank, narrowly escaped bankruptcy, twenty-five grand in debt and pregnant with our second child, and once again, Bill's boss was threatening to sack him.

"He's an even bigger twat than the guy at the company here was. Honestly, why do I always get landed with them?"

I didn't have an answer to that. All I could think about was our plans to move to France after the baby was born, and whether or not we'd still be able to go through with them. I didn't want to show Bill how worried I was, though. He was clearly really stressed, and I didn't want to make things worse. I bit my tongue and put my faith in him to sort things out.

Bill returned to France that Sunday night, and I was almost relieved. The weekend hadn't been good. Bill was tense and so was I. I'd tried my hardest to reassure him, but I needed reassurance myself and I wasn't really getting any. If I brought up the subject of the loan, he just dismissed it and told me we'd pay it. How, I didn't know. He must have had a plan.

* * *

I didn't sleep well that night. Something felt wrong. The next day the pains were back. This time they were stronger than before. I was scared. I called the Doctor and she came to see me.

"OK Sarah," she'd said. "I really don't think we have a choice now. You're going to have to go into hospital until we get this under control. We need to get you to thirty four weeks, and at this rate, it isn't going to happen. You need one hundred percent bed rest, and steroids to get the baby's lungs to develop in case it comes early. How long do you need to get everything organised?" I looked at Lucy, and tears filled my eyes. How the hell was I going to be able to go into hospital? My baby was ten months old and she needed her mummy. Her daddy was miles away working, and we simply couldn't afford for him to take time off. My friends were rallying around, but Lucy needed constant care, and my friends had their own lives to lead. I felt helpless and scared. But I knew that for the sake of my unborn baby I would have to take the doctor's advice. Lucy would have to be OK, even though I couldn't bear the thought of being parted from her. I called my mum, and she immediately arranged to get the next flight to Switzerland. It was a big relief; at least I knew Lucy would be in loving and capable hands. As soon as I called Bill, he too arranged to get the next flight back. Even though he was paid on a daily rate, and we could ill afford for him to take time off, especially now the situation with his boss was so awkward, I was grateful he was coming home. I needed my husband with me to reassure me.

I went into hospital and was put in a side room on the maternity ward. There were new born babies everywhere, and this really brought my situation home to me. I was ninety percent certain I had another little girl in there, and I was determined she was going to stay put until she was healthy enough to come out. Once I was hooked up to a drip to slow the contractions, I had time to really reflect on things. I was bed-bound now after all. I looked at my pregnant belly, and for the first time I connected to the little girl who was inside me. I'd been neglecting her in recent weeks, and in that moment I cried for her and asked her to forgive me. I'd been so caught up in everything that had been happening. I'd barely had time to register that I was pregnant. The shock at discovering I was carrying another child had quickly been overridden by a wealth of other problems, and I hadn't given any thought to this little girl whilst I'd been so distracted with Lucy, Bill, and the financial and emotional stresses and strains. Even when I'd had the warning signs I hadn't really slowed down. How could I have been so thoughtless? Lying there in the hospital, I bonded with my unborn baby girl, and I vowed to her that I would never let her down again.

* * *

Once my mum arrived in Switzerland I was able to relax a bit more. Bill wasn't coping well with everything that was happening. He didn't seem to cope well under pressure. I think he felt helpless and out of control, and it wasn't something he dealt with well. Lucy was confused and inevitably picking up on his stress. My mum's arrival was a godsend, and enabled us all to relax with the situation a bit more. On my insistence, Bill returned to France the next week.

"You need to go back," I'd said. "We can't afford for you to lose this job. Lucy and I are fine; my mum can take care of us. You need to go back and fight for your contract. Please Bill, don't lose this contract." Reluctantly, he'd returned.

"He's not looking well!" my mum had said to me after he'd gone. "He's gained weight and he looks really grey. He's stressed out. He's manic. He almost crashed the car on the way to the hospital today. He was driving like a maniac, with Lucy in the back!"

She was really concerned about him. I too had noticed his weight gain. It had been a steady thing, but more or less since the wedding, he'd been piling on the pounds. In the early days, he proclaimed to be sporty. We would cycle, inline skate and swim regularly. He'd never had a great physique. He liked his food and wine too much for that, but he did seem to take pride in his appearance and he would spend a great deal of time on grooming. Since the wedding, though, it had all changed. I was quite into keeping fit, and have always been very figure conscious, so I was disappointed when Bill started to let his figure go. In an effort to encourage him, I'd spent well over a thousand francs on a year's membership of the local gym. He'd gone once. I was frustrated about this, not least because it had cost me so much money, but also because I felt he didn't seem inclined to make an effort anymore.

"He's prime candidate for a heart attack!" my mum had said. "He's overweight, stressed, and he drinks too much. You need to talk to him Sarah, for his sake, and the sake of your kids!"

So I spoke to him, in the gentlest way I could. I told him how worried we were, and asked him to get himself checked out.

"Please, do it for the kids and me. We love you and we need you. We need you to take care of yourself so you can take care of us.""

"OK", he'd agreed, and he went for a check-up. It came back all clear, but the doctor had recommended that Bill take sleeping tablets, to get him over the stressful time. Bill rarely took the tablets though, only when I had insisted. Sleeping tablets were for wimps.

After eight days in the hospital I was allowed to go home. The contractions had eased, and there were no more signs of imminent labour. I'd made a pact with my little girl (we'd decided to call her Alice), and she'd agreed to stay put as long as I took things easy. I was still not allowed to be on my feet very much, and lifting Lucy was strictly forbidden, so my mum kindly offered to stay with us for the duration. It was such a weight off my mind, and something for which I'll be eternally grateful to her.

My mum and I have always been close, but in those weeks at the end of the pregnancy, we bonded even more. We settled into our own little routine with Lucy, and we enjoyed long chats during the evenings. It was a magical time, despite the stressful circumstances.

For Bill, it was not so much fun. He didn't like having another adult in the house, especially as the other adult was my mother, somebody I looked up to and whose opinions and advice I respected. He clearly felt like a spare part when he came home for the weekends. And despite him bringing expensive duty free gifts to my mother on almost every return trip, I could sense he would much rather have she wasn't there. Not least because her encouragement and guidance saw me gaining even more confidence in myself as a mother.

* * *

The day after her first birthday, Lucy took ill. It was a run of the mill gastric bug, but she was violently sick and lost a lot of fluids. Whenever anything happened to Lucy, Bill went into panic mode. It was the only situation I ever saw him flapping, but it happened regularly. If she slipped whilst crawling, he'd instantly be there, sweeping her up in his arms and soothing her with "There, there, Daddy's here". He went into her room every morning he was home, even though she was still sleeping. He'd pick her up, because he wanted to the first person she saw. He would constantly check her temperature and her breathing, regardless of her state of health. This time was the first time she'd been really ill whilst he was present, and he was a nervous wreck. She was running a slight fever. We'd opened her window and put a fan in her room, but she was restless and crying.

"We need to call a doctor", Bill had said. It was midnight, and Bill, my mum and myself, were all in Lucy's room. Bill cradled her on his knee, mopping her brow with a flannel, much to her dismay. I was reluctant to call a doctor. She was poorly, but I didn't feel she needed a Doctor. I felt she needed rest. Being jogged up and down on her daddy's knee wasn't helping. She needed to be in bed, sleeping it off.

"Go and get the Doctor's number, Sarah!" he ordered me.

"Well, OK, but what am I going to say? I don't think there's anything a Doctor can really do."

"I agree with Sarah," my mum had chipped in, only to be shot daggers by Bill.

"For Christ's sakes, just give me the phone and I'll do it myself," he'd snapped. "You think you're a good mother, yet you can't even do this for your daughter", he spat.

"Now then!" My mother rarely got involved in arguments, but she jumped to my defense. "That was below the belt!"

I was shocked and angered. How dare he question my skills as a mother? Lucy didn't need a Doctor! I decided to dig my heels in.

"Fine, you call if you must, but I'm not going to, because I don't believe she needs it. She needs fluids and rest. Put her down, for goodness sake; you're making her more upset by manhandling her the whole time!" He shot me a look I'll never forget. He wasn't used to me asserting myself when it came to Lucy. He put her back in her cot, and sat with her for the rest of the night.

* * *

I was keeping my half of the deal I'd made with Alice, and she was keeping hers. The contractions had stopped now, and she was growing normally inside me. I talked to her every night and sang softly to her. I told my mum what we were going to call her. I felt I'd truly bonded with her before I even laid eyes on her. We got to full term, thirty-seven weeks, and she decided to remain put. I became more active, to encourage her to come into the world and meet us. She obliged, two weeks after Lucy turned one, at thirty-eight weeks exactly.

Alice's birth was much more straightforward than Lucy's had been, and I was up on my feet again within a day or two. This time it wasn't as overwhelming, and I didn't feel the fog that had descended after Lucy's birth. Once again, it was love at first sight. I was completely in awe of this little blue-eyed creature in my arms. I couldn't put her down. When I looked into her face, it was like greeting a dear old friend. She had such wisdom in her eyes, and such a knowing look about her. I felt like I'd known this little girl all my life. I had no inhibitions this time around. I knew it was going to be hard work, especially as I was going to be on my own with two such young babies, but I wasn't scared any more. I knew what I was doing with Alice. I didn't need Bill to show me how to change a nappy or bathe her. I felt confidence and pride. I never knew I had it in me, and it made me feel good. I was so engrossed with Alice, and getting home and into a routine, I barely noticed that Bill wasn't as pushy this time as he'd been with Lucy. I assumed he just realised I was better prepared this time, and was letting me get on with taking care of my new born. I felt he was giving me some space, and not being so overbearing. I also assumed he was so wrapped up in other things, he simply didn't have time to get as excited about this new arrival as he had about our last. It didn't occur to me that he wasn't really that interested in Alice.

Chapter Nine

A Move to Somewhere New

And so began a whole new routine for me. Two weeks after Alice's birth, my mum returned to England, and with Bill already back in France, I found myself on my own with my two little girls. It was a period of relative calm. I had expected things to be tough for me, alone with two babies, but the reality was much easier than I had imagined it would be. We quickly settled into a routine, and despite the predictable tiredness, I coped much better than I had anticipated. Even Bill commented on how well I was doing without him. Rare praise, indeed.

Now that Alice was safely in the world, it was time to think about the future. Thanks to the intervention of Bill's friend in Human Resources with the company in France, Bill's relationship with his boss has eased, and he was being allowed to complete the current contract. His friend had also managed to line up a second contract in a different department, which meant that for the rest of the year at least, our income was secured. Bill was also extremely confident that the work would extend once the next contract was complete. Having a best friend in HR certainly had its advantages. We were therefore able to start planning the move to France, safe in the knowledge that contracts would be in constant future supply. Bill and his friend Tom seemed to go back a long way. He was the only 'old' friend of Bill's who had remained in touch with him. We had stayed with Tom and his wife in France on a couple of occasions, and Tom had been Bill's best man at the wedding. Tom and his wife were the only other people I'd met who had known Sofia. They didn't talk about her much though, and they certainly didn't pass judgment on Bill when he first took me to France to meet them. They were certainly not as disapproving as Bill's other friends who had known Sofia. Tom drove a Porsche, which had previously belonged to Bill. Bill explained to me one day that he'd sold it to Tom for a knock-down price, in order to 'prevent *her* getting *her* hands on it,' ('her' being, of course, Sofia.)

I often wondered about this transaction. Why would you sell a car for less than half its worth, simply to prevent your wife from taking ownership of it? Despite what Bill had told me about his trusting Sofia, and his total shock upon discovering her financial deception, he must have at least suspected her of something, otherwise why sell the car to his friend? This, coupled with Bill's story about 'filtering' money off their German company to stash in an anonymous offshore account without Sofia's knowledge, often left me questioning whether Bill had been entirely truthful when he'd told me the breakdown of the marriage had been amicable. Still, Tom and Bill shared great camaraderie, and I always enjoyed spending time with them. He was also a great friend to have, not least because without Tom's help and support, Bill and I would be financially high and dry by now. We handed our notice in on the Swiss apartment, and the countdown to the move began.

This was a bittersweet time for me. On the one hand, I was excited about the move to a new country, and beginning a new life. I felt as though our lives had been on hold for so long now, and I was keen to finally begin our life as a proper family, just Bill, the girls and me. On the other hand, I had this sense of overwhelming loss. I was just finding my feet as a mother of two. I loved the freedom I had being on my own with the girls. I was starting to feel secure in my relationships with friends again, after the gossip and finger pointing of the past twelve months. I felt I had cemented so many good friendships. I was truly proud at how people had rallied around me during the problems with my second pregnancy. I felt we had once again been accepted amongst the group of friends, and I was grateful to them all for helping me get back on my feet again after such a difficult time. I felt safe for the first time in a long time, and I didn't want that feeling to go away. I knew we had no choice, though. I'd married a consultant, and I knew I had to go with Bill where the work was, in order to keep our family together. I resolved that life in France was our future, and I threw myself into focusing on making a life there.

During this time, Bill was still doing his usual 'wheeling and dealing 'on the side. I say 'wheeling and dealing,' but the reality was it was 'talking and talking,' because none of the 'deals' actually came to fruition. Bill always seemed to miss out by a hare's whisker. Somebody in the chain would always 'fuck up,' as Bill put it, and he'd narrowly miss out on his multi-million pay-out. The aircraft deal had fallen through when the 'wanker' in the Middle East had gone behind Bill's back at the last minute, and taken his custom elsewhere, despite Bill having spent hours and hours compiling detailed pricing information and presentations. Basically, the guy had ripped Bill off, or so he said.

"Well, why do you do all this work for people upfront?" I'd ventured to ask one day. "You shouldn't do anything without some sort of agreement in place to ensure you get paid for your time, surely?"

He'd sighed.

"Because, darling, it just doesn't work like that. It's an unwritten rule in business, a gentleman's agreement. In order to win the contract, I have to do work upfront to show I'm the person they need on board."

"Well, to be honest I can't really see the point," I'd argued. "Twice now you've been on the verge of a big deal; you've invested weeks and even months of your time, then nothing has come of it."

"That's just the way it is," he'd snapped. "You have to keep at it; one of the deals will come to fruition."

Personally, I wished he'd just focus on the contract for which he was being paid, and stop chasing multi-million pound deals which never came to anything, but I resolved that this was the way Bill was, always chasing the 'big one.' And of course I'd be lying if I didn't say that the thought of him finally landing one of these big bucks deals was really appealing to me too.

During that summer, Bill had been scouring the area close to his office for a new place for us to live. He'd been to look at several houses, but nothing remotely suitable had come up. In July, we were sent an advertisement from an agency that was renting a cottage in the remote rural village where Bill's house was. It seemed almost as though it was meant to be. A four-bedroomed cottage, in the grounds of a chateau, two minutes' walk from Bill's dad and step mum. As soon as he went to see the place, Bill was sold on it.

"It's just amazing," he'd enthused. "It's perfect. It's a bit rural, but the area is full of ex-pats, so there'll be no problem integrating. Obviously it's going to be a long commute to work for me, but at least you and the girls will be close to family, and I'm sure you'll have no problem making friends."

It seemed like a perfect solution, and Bill's enthusiasm was contagious. I really started to like the idea of living in the grounds of a chateau in rural France. And I loved the idea of Lucy and Alice having grandparents close by. We could be a proper family at last! It all sounded so romantic! I really started to look forward to the move. Bill's project ended that summer, and he had a three-week holiday before starting his new contract in another department of the company.

During that time, he turned fifty, and I organised a surprise garden party for him at one of the local lakeside hotels. He was in his element at the party. He loved nothing more than being the centre of attention, and after the difficulties of the past twelve months, it was clear that even he was relieved to still be able to bask in his popularity. I'd dressed the girls up especially for the occasion. Lucy looked a picture in her summer dress and bonnet. Bill barely let her stray from his side, taking her to say hello to all his guests, and getting her to demonstrate her limited vocabulary and new-found walking skills. He was a very proud father.

Alice was of course only a couple of months old at the time, and I was still feeding her myself, so she remained close to me in her pram, whilst I helped to organise the food and drinks. Bill revelled in the attention, and when it came to opening his presents, he took full advantage of the fact he had a large and captive audience. He opened each present one by one, making a drawn out speech with each time. It actually became painful to watch, as people were clearly losing concentration and wanted to get back to the party. But this was typical Bill behaviour. He was constantly holding court, lapping up attention, and reaffirming at every opportunity just what a popular and inspiring man he was. I dismissed the sinking feeling I got in my stomach whilst listening to Bill address his audience. I dismissed the feeling I got when I looked around at their faces to see mostly faux interest and some mocking disdain. I certainly dismissed the feeling I suddenly got, that people might actually feel sorry for me. And when we all went back to our house to continue the party, I ignored the feeling of horror and embarrassment I felt, when a drunken Bill produced glossy brochures of machine guns and grenades, and announced to our incredulous friends, that he was about to make millions by clinching an arms deal with an EU member state.

September came, and it was time to leave our lives in Switzerland behind, and begin the next chapter, in France. For over a month now we had been living in chaos, with packing boxes everywhere. I had been trying my best not to think about the fact that we were leaving the place I loved, and all my friends behind, and tried instead to keep looking forwards, and get happy about the new life ahead of us. The girls were being amazing. Lucy was unsettled over the move, she didn't understand what was happening, but she was happy as long as either Bill or I were close to her. Alice was a pure delight. She was such a contented little baby and never complained about anything. She was still so small, and I was of course the person who was closest to her. She had slept in the guest room of our apartment with me, since her birth. The guest bedroom was next to the nursery where Lucy was, and as the main bedroom was on a different level, it had seemed easier for me to simply move closer to the girls. Bill remained in the master bedroom when he came home at weekends. This of course meant that all the night feeding of Alice had been left to me, which resulted in Bill taking more care of Lucy whilst he was around, and leaving Alice to me.

* * *

The day we left Switzerland was cold, dark and rainy. It was so depressing. I'd got hideously drunk the night before, and ended up in a puddle of tears, desperate to stay in

95

Switzerland; yet knowing we had to leave. I was very down and upset, and feeling extremely delicate. The journey was a complete nightmare. Lucy began vomiting at about the half-way point, and continued for the rest of the journey. Every thirty minutes or so, projectile vomiting; the poor little might was very ill, and by the time we arrived at Bill's house in France we were all completely exhausted.

Bill's dad and step mum hadn't seemed as enamoured with the idea of us moving so close to them as we'd hoped. I wondered if they felt slightly threatened. They'd lived in Bill's house for almost ten years now, and had invested a great deal of effort and money into maintaining it, and decorating it to their tastes. I'd asked Bill to reassure them that we had no plans to move into the house, or indeed sell it. I wanted to reassure them that the roof over their heads was safe, and that we'd moved there simply because we had wanted to be close to family, and for the girls to experience having grandparents close by. I'm not sure if Bill ever did make any effort to reassure them, though, because the reception, whilst pleasant enough, was certainly not what I was hoping for upon our arrival in France. It had been our plan to stay with them for two or three days, until we'd had a chance to take delivery of the furniture, and get the new cottage sorted out. It didn't work out like that, though, because after only one night, Bill's step mum was hurrying us along to get ourselves into the new place, despite the boxes still not being unpacked, and the babies' beds not even being assembled yet. It was perplexing to say the least. They seemed very keen for us not to be in their house, to the point that when Bill went up to collect a few things, he found his step mother putting the travel cots and children's bags out in her driveway ready to be collected.

I tried not to let this upset me too much. Bill didn't have a close relationship with his father and step mum, and it was mainly on my encouragement that he'd had regular contact with them at all in the years since I'd known him. Bill had told me stories about his father, and how he'd been a brutal man who had bullied his wife and terrorised his children. When Bill's mother was dying from cancer and in hospital, Bill's father had struck up a relationship with his now stepmother, and (in Bill's eyes) had neglected his duties to his dying wife, in favour of pursuing his new relationship. This had inevitably led to a strained relationship between Bill and his father, and of course his stepmother.

And so we found ourselves exhausted, in our new house, surrounded by boxes. We opened a bottle of bubbly to toast our new lives, but I wasn't able to drink mine; I was starting to feel ill. That second night in France, our first in the new cottage, I spent with my head down the toilet. Clearly, whatever Lucy had suffered, had been contagious. I got no sleep at all; I felt like death warmed up, and I could barely move because of the pain. The next morning, Bill brought the girls into the room with me and disappeared downstairs to unpack some boxes in the garage. I couldn't cope with the babies. Lucy was running around crying, and Alice needed feeding and changing. When Bill came back in, I implored him to help me.

97

"I can barely move," I'd said. "I don't think I can get out of bed."

"Well, we need to go to the supermarket. We've got no food in, and it's Saturday; if we don't stock up now, we'll have nothing to eat all weekend."

"Please, Bill, can you take the kids with you? I need to sleep or I'm not going to get better." Bill sighed.

"I'll take Lucy."

"Can't you take Alice? I don't feel well enough to look after her properly."

"No, I can't take her," he snapped at me. "How do you expect me to manage around a supermarket with both of them in toe?"

"The same way I always manage?" I'd sighed. He ignored the comment, and left, taking just Lucy with him. He was gone for about four hours. I forced myself to get up so I could look after Alice. Every movement hurt. It was one hell of a long day.

That night, it was Bill's turn to be ill. Like me, he spent the night in the bathroom throwing up. The next day, I was feeling slightly more human again, so I got up with the girls. I didn't see Bill at all that day; he never moved from the bed, not even when I took him fluids and medication. That afternoon, I sat on my own, in a cottage in the middle of nowhere. There was no phone to call my mum, and Bill was in bed upstairs. I felt rejected by Bill's parents, and apart from the kid's presence, I felt lonely. This felt wrong, all wrong.

Chapter Ten

A Dark Time

The first month was a complete nightmare. I don't think I'd ever felt so low up until that point of my life. Bill would leave the house at seven each day, and only return between seven and eight in the evening. I had no car, and there were no buses from this backwater to any amenities. I was left alone with Lucy and Alice, unable to even go to the local supermarket. What made it worse was that Bill's father and stepmother seemed completely disinterested in us all. I had hoped we would be in and out of each other's houses for coffee, and that she would at least offer to give me the occasional lift to the local town for shopping. As it happened, she only took us once, after I'd asked her out of sheer desperation to get out of the house. I really couldn't put my finger on their apparent hostility towards us. I tried to speak to Bill about it, to see if he could maybe have a word with them and reassure them that we weren't after the house; I was convinced they still believed we wanted to throw them out of their home. But Bill was equally disinterested. It didn't bother him at all. He was unsympathetic to my plight. He didn't seem to realise how very alone and isolated I felt. It was OK for him. He was socialising all day with other adults. He was getting conversation and intellectual stimulation. I, on the other hand, was stuck at home with no means of escape. I couldn't even take the girls for a walk; the roads were so rural, there were ditches on either side, and the French drivers would careen along at frightening speeds. I didn't want to risk taking the children out at all. Depression came.

Money was still tight, despite the fact that our rent in France was so much lower than it had been in Switzerland. The move had been costly, and we'd had to furnish the house with white goods; things which are normally included in the price of the house. Not only this, but we were making large monthly payments from the 'wedding' debt, and now it was clear we were going to need a second car, if my sanity and the welfare of the girls was to be saved.

At the beginning of November, Bill procured a small car to use for work, leaving me with the family four-by-four. This made things much more bearable for me, as I was finally going to be able to get about and make some friends. I joined a mother and baby group for ex-pats, and life slowly started to improve.

The problem with Bill's parents seemed to be worsening, though, and in November it became glaringly apparent that things were definitely not normal. My parents were over for a week, and despite being only a five minutes' walk away, Bill's parents made no effort to come and see us, or invite us to theirs.

"This is all really weird," I'd said to my mum. "What do you think it could be? I just don't get it!"

"I have no idea," my mum had replied "I'm so envious of them, having their granddaughters living this close. I simply can't believe they would not be interested in being part of their lives."

I was hurt and upset on behalf of Lucy and Alice. I had no idea why Bill's parents were behaving like this towards us. There was no one event that I could remember, where we may have upset of offended them somehow. It kept niggling at me. I recalled earlier in the year, Bill had received a call from them one weekend whilst he was home in Switzerland, and they'd asked him for money towards roof repairs on his house. The figure they had asked for was in the region of six thousand Euros. Clearly, there was no way we could afford it. This request came at the time when we'd only just escaped the bankruptcy proceedings, and we were negotiating repayments of the 'wedding' loan Bill had taken out.

After the phone call, in which Bill had told them he would 'think about it,' I implored him to come clean with them.

"You can't just say no without giving them reasons," I'd said. "You have to tell them about Sofia's betrayal and the subsequent mess she has left you with. They'll understand there's no way we can afford to help them out right now."

"We shouldn't have to anyway," he'd said, "They have lived there rent free for the past decade. The deal was that they would look after the house and pay for its upkeep."

"Yes, Bill, but they are pensioners, and it's clear they've invested a lot into this. You should at least show that you're willing to help. And anyway, you can't really blame them for asking. We don't exactly look as though we're strapped for cash. We've got a gorgeous Swiss apartment and a brand new luxury car. Clearly they think we can afford it. You have to be honest with them."

And so, he'd told them that Sofia had taken out a massive bank loan prior to her death, and that, as a result of default on that loan, we had narrowly escaped bankruptcy. They accepted the story, and were aware that we'd seen the Notaire to try and transfer ownership of the house into my name. With that, we'd assumed the situation was resolved, until now.

At the beginning of December they called us and asked us if we could go to the house for a 'meeting,' it sounded a bit ominous. And it was. His stepmother did most of the talking.

"Basically, we need to get our money out of the house," she'd said. "We've worked out what we spent so far, and we think that twenty thousand Euros is a fair request."

Bill's chin nearly hit the table.

"Twenty grand! There's no way you've spent that much!" he exclaimed. I was horrified. How could they realistically expect Bill to pay that to them, when not only had they lived for ten years rent free, but they knew the financial dire straits we were in!

"That is easily what we've spent Bill," his stepmother retaliated. "This place was practically derelict when we moved in. We've ploughed all our savings into this place and turned it into a marketable house. We've had it valued, and you'll still be making money on it if you sell it now and pay us what you owe us."

"What I owe you? I think you'll find I don't owe you anything," Bill said calmly, almost smiling.

"We have a contract which we drew up when we moved in; it clearly states that you will pay for structural repairs. We were responsible only for the upkeep. We've had major work done on the roof, and to the general structure. We've also completely overhauled the garden. This IS what you owe us Bill."

Bill just shook his head. I wanted the ground to open up and swallow me. How could his parents be like this with us, knowing all that had happened? I was incredulous.

"You'd better bloody well give us the money!" Bill's dad was shouting. "Please don't shout at me," Bill had replied to his father, as he turned to his stepmother.

"I'll have to think about it. Maybe I can help you out if you're struggling for cash. I'll happily help you to work through your finances and see if we can work out a plan. But I will not be paying you twenty thousand Euros, and I will not be selling the house. We will transfer the ownership into

Sarah's name, and you can continue to live here for as long as you wish. Come on Sarah, we're leaving."

And with that, we left. Now it was clear why they'd been strange with us all this time. They were gearing themselves up to demand money from us! I felt sick. How could they do this? Why did things like this keep happening to us? How could Bill's own parents turn on him like this? Did they have no heart?

Later that day, Bill received a letter through the post box. It was from his stepmother explaining how deeply hurt and disappointed they both were with him, and saying she felt Bill had used and betrayed them. She said she'd loved him like her own son, yet this was the thanks she got. She said she wanted nothing more to do with us. I can't begin to describe how devastated I felt. We had come here to begin a new life. We'd come to this village purely because it was where they were, and they were my little girl's grandparents! How could they turn their backs on my little girls? All over money? Why did everything in our lives always come down to money? Why did Bill seem to attract these mercenary people into his life?

"Cheeky bastards!" he'd exclaimed. "How the hell dare they! The house was NOT derelict when they moved in. Far from it! It needed a bit of re-wiring, a bit of plumbing, and the roof needed work. Nothing else! I'll be surprised if that roof cost six grand to fix, and everything else was done either by them or by me when I was down! They bought all the materials locally; it could hardly have broken the bank. Twenty grand my arse! I can't believe they're so bloody ungrateful. I gave them a roof over their heads when they were in need, and I've never charged them a penny. Now they come to me trying to leech off me. Well tough. It isn't going to happen!" I was at a loss to explain it all. I wholeheartedly agreed with Bill that they were being unreasonable. I had no reason to doubt what he was telling me, and it certainly didn't appear that the house had really had twenty thousand spent on it. But of course, I hadn't seen the house to begin with, so I only had his word for it. And as usual, I took him at his word. I pleaded with Bill not to let this one go, this was too important, they were family.

"Please, let's try to reason with them!" I'd implored. "We'll sit them down and try to work something out. Obviously we can't afford to pay them anything at the moment, not with our financial situation, but maybe we can arrange to subsidise them somewhat, and help them get back on their feet financially. We can help them to manage any debts they have now, and perhaps give them a small monthly subsidy until the house is sold. Once the house has been sold, we'll give them a lump sum, what do you think?"

He clearly didn't want to even meet them halfway, but after much persuasion on my part, he finally agreed to try and talk to them. He arranged for us to go up there one Sunday after lunch. After some stilted small talk, Bill and his stepmother finally got onto the subject of finances.

"We agree to sell the house, as soon as we've changed it into Sarah's name, otherwise we lose half its value to Sofia's relatives. The paperwork and the sale could take months, even years, so in the meantime, I'm prepared to sit with you to discuss how you can overcome the current cash flow problem. I can't give you much in the way of cash, but I might be able to help you with some ideas."

"Are you prepared to give us back the money we have invested in this house?" asked his stepmother.

"No, I'm not, not the full amount. You've lived here rent free for ten years, and that needs to be taken into account."

With that, Bill's father was on his feet and yelling.

"You low-down, cheap, bastard!" he screamed. "You've been good for nothing your entire life, and you'll never amount to anything. From the moment you were chucked out of the RAF for smoking pot, you've been a failure at everything you've done. You've leeched off other people and now you've leeched off us!" Bill stood up and met his father's gaze head on.

"I'm not listening to this," he said softly. And with that, he turned and left. I couldn't believe it. Bill's father was screeching and waving his fists by now; his stepmother was making moves to try and restrain him. And Bill had gone! Lucy was crying, and poor little Alice was staring wide-eyed at Bill's father. I gathered the kids up as fast as I could, and shoved them out of the door and away from Bill's wild and threatening father. I was shaking from head to foot, and so was Bill.

"That's it," he said. "No more. They get nothing from me now."

* * *

The next week, Bill went to see the Notaire and instructed him to put the house up for sale.

"What about transferring ownership?" I asked him. "We don't have to," he'd replied. "He can put the house on the market, and when we get an offer, we claim we couldn't contact the next of kin." He made a 'wink' face.

"What about your parents?" I'd asked.

"What about them? You heard what was said. It could take months to sell the house, and if that happens, we can make them an offer. In the meantime, they get no say in the matter." And that was how it was left. Christmas was just around the corner, and we'd just had a major bust up with the only family we had in the immediate vicinity. What a year it had been! I wasn't sure which had been worse: the beginning of the year, with bailiffs and court orders, or the end of the year, stuck in the middle of nowhere and estranged from Bill's family.

Surely next year could only get better?

Chapter Eleven

Changing Fortunes, Changing Feelings

After a quiet Christmas at the cottage, just the four of us, we returned to the UK for New Year. It was lovely to be back in the 'civilised' world again, and I realised whilst we were there that I was absolutely dreading returning to France. The last three months had been utter hell. I hated the house, the location, the feeling of being so utterly isolated, and now I hated the fact that we had yet again become embroiled in a major row. Resentment had started to build in me. I tried to ignore it, but it was there, in the pit of my stomach, eating away. One night, we'd been out drinking with friends. I'd got into a complete state. Once I'd started, I couldn't stop, and I was stupidly drunk. This was not the state that happy, contented people get into. This was the state somebody drinks herself into when she is hiding, trying to block something out. The truth comes out when you're drunk. I was sick, and Bill had to clean up the mess. The next day, he told me that I'd been sitting on top of the toilet in my parents' bathroom watching him clear up the mess.

"If looks could kill, I'd have been a dead man," he'd said. "You had a look of hatred in your eyes."

I couldn't believe it. I felt so guilty. He was my husband, how could I hate him and treat him with such disrespect? He'd mopped up after me, a sign of true love and dedication.

I hated myself for treating him that way. The guilt lasted days, and during that time, I was overly attentive and kind to my husband. This was to become an all too familiar pattern from now on.

* * *

Upon our return, we were met with the next major blow. We had a letter from the Notaire. In it, he wrote that he had received a letter from Bill's father, which stated that Sofia's mother was indeed still alive, and provided contact details for her. Not only this, but the letter included contact details for Sofia's half sisters and brother from Australia. The Notaire warned that proceeding with the house sale could result in criminal proceedings, as Bill had been trying to bypass the inheritance laws. He requested urgent instruction on how to proceed.

"I don't believe it!" Bill was raging; he was shaking from head to foot.

"Those bastards! They have deliberately tried to sabotage the house sale. They have done this on purpose to hurt us financially! I cannot believe how they could be so nasty!"

I couldn't believe it either. I was enraged! How could parents do that to their own child? He'd explained to them about what Sofia had done. Her mother was living in a house paid for with Bill's money. That he had a massive debt hanging over him because of her, and that her mother knew this. They had deliberately sabotaged Bill's only piece of security, and for what? What did they hope to achieve? I wept again for my girls. How could their grandparents do this to them? No matter what they thought of Bill, surely the children's future should be paramount to them? How could they want to destroy it? How could they? I felt sick to my stomach. I cannot describe the desperation I felt. I couldn't believe that people could be so cruel. This was a complete disaster. Another complete disaster. How much more could we withstand? Later that day, we had a visit from our landlady, the Chateau owner.

"I've had a letter," she said. "It's from your parents, Bill."

 When we'd moved into the cottage, Bill's parents had stood as guarantors for our rent. This is standard practice in France. The letter was effectively withdrawing their guarantee, and explaining to our landlady that Bill had a history of financial problems and was currently 'financially unstable'.

"So now they're trying to get us evicted as well! Unreal!" Bill had shouted.

"That's it, it's over," he said. "They can rot now for all I care. I'm going to evict them."

And that's exactly what he did. He went to see a solicitor and served them with an eviction notice later that same week. He did this with my full support. I was incredulous at what they had tried to do to us, and I was furious on behalf of my husband and babies. I just couldn't understand what they had hoped to achieve. Bill had offered them an allowance and a small settlement from the sale of the house. Surely that would have been better than nothing? Now, they had contacted Sofia's relatives, knowing what Sofia had done, and effectively put the kibosh on any profit from the house, cutting off their only hope of ever getting their money back. Were they crazy? I was so angry I would have happily seen them thrown on the street myself. But Bill was determined, and despite them trying to argue that they had a contract, Bill was ruthless. I'd never seen him act this way before. I assumed he was driven by hurt and anger at yet another betrayal. He was going to stop at nothing, even if the legal fees were more than we could afford. He left them no choice but to give in. They had two months to pack up and get out.

Once again, I found myself ostracized by the locals. It was a tiny village, and everybody knew everybody else. Clearly they sided with Bill's parents, who had lived there for years, and we were the ones who were in the wrong. They couldn't have known the truth, so I told myself it was inevitable they take sides with his parents. Bill wasn't bothered. He never was by this sort of thing. But I was deeply upset. One day, I'd taken the rubbish up to the main bins in the village. One of the locals had parked his car in the road outside his house, and was standing talking to his neighbour. I drove up in the four by four, which was too wide to get past. He walked out into the middle of the road, and just stood there, staring at me. I had no choice but to reverse down the narrow street, and take a detour around the village. It was a horrible experience, and once again I was in tears. I wanted to go back to Switzerland. I missed my friends, the crisp clean countryside, our beautiful apartment, and most of all, the language. I couldn't speak good French, and I hated not being able to communicate with people. This would have been bad enough by itself, but now we were once again the butt of gossip, yet this time it was even worse. This time we were the evil and ruthless rich people who were turfing their own parents out onto the street, in order to cash in on the sale of the house that those pensioners had sunk their life savings into. It was almost unbearable, and were it not for my ex-pat friends at the mother and baby group, I might have gone completely mad.

Bill was back to working long hours. He was now on another project and once again there was conflict between him and his superior. He became more and more distant. He was sleeping in the guest room now. We'd hardly shared the same bed since Alice was born. It was for practical reasons at first, but as time had gone by it became through choice. I loved Bill, but I didn't want to share a bed with him anymore. He snored like mad and kept me awake, and in turn I would become tired and irritable. It made sense that if we were both to get a good night's sleep, we should sleep apart. This was how I reconciled it to myself. I blocked out the fact that I simply couldn't bear the thought of him touching me. He would get up at around six in the morning, shower and get dressed. He'd leave the house at seven and was rarely home before eight thirty in the evening. On the rare occasions he did get home earlier, he would barely have time for the kids. When he did have time for the kids, it was always Lucy he gravitated towards, never Alice. It broke my heart to watch.

Alice was now crawling around, and becoming her own little person. She adored her daddy, yet he barely seemed to notice she was there. I remember clearly how one evening, he came home from work and Alice was sitting in the middle of the carpet, surrounded by toys. As the door opened and he stepped inside, her head turned to him and her eyes lit up. She beamed at him, but he didn't even look at her. Instead, he stepped right over her in order to get to Lucy, who was sitting with me on the sofa. He swept Lucy up in his arms and then spun her around, laughing and cuddling her. Little Alice's face said a million things to me, and I almost wept for her.

"Alice wants to say hello to daddy too, don't you Alice?" I said as I went over to her and stroked her cheek. Bill turned and looked over his shoulder at Alice. He put Lucy down and bent down to pat Alice's head.

"Hello sweetheart," he said. Then turned and headed into his room to take off his coat.

It wasn't just Alice who was being pushed out. It was me too. Bill was pending all his time sitting in his office. He was apparently working on another 'deal' that was going to earn big bucks, and this was his reason for locking himself in his office all evening.

Our relationship was starting to unravel, and we both knew it. I wanted us to be a family, but it was always me who seemed to make the effort. Whenever did anything as a family, unless it was me who instigated it. If we were to spend a day at a zoo, or a play park, I had to organise it myself, and basically just tell Bill we were going out. He'd 'happily' come along, but he'd certainly never volunteer it. Even at the weekends, we'd barely see him. There was always something happening on the internet that was far more important.

There was a fog descending around me again, and that feeling in the pit of my stomach was becoming chronic. It was rot, and it was spreading. I couldn't ignore its existence, as much as I tried to deny to myself it was there. At this time, I had another shock coming to me. One day I opened my mailbox to discover an email from a person called Rich. It had come into my account via the website Bill had set up for our wedding. I saw from the address that it was from Australia, and a quick read of the mail made me realise immediately who it was from.

'Bill, are you still out there? I'm thinking about you and hoping to catch up with you very soon. Why didn't you contact me to tell me about Sofia, Bill? You knew her family didn't have my contact details, but you did. You could have let me know yet you chose not to? Why Bill? It took them months to track me down to give me the news. I couldn't even go to my sisters' funeral, all because of you, Bill.

Why did you disappear, Bill? Were you running away from something? Were you scared Bill? Are you still? You should be, Bill. I stood at my sister's grave last month. It was a cold and rainy day. I stood at her grave and I vowed I would sort this out for her, Bill. I vowed I would get some answers. And get them I will.

Cheers

Rich'

I sat staring at it for about ten minutes. I was in a trance. I felt sick to my stomach. What the hell was all this about? I shivered. It was like an ice cold bolt hit me from the blue. That voice was there again, whispering in my ear.

"The bubble has burst, the bubble has burst." I ignored it and forwarded the mail to Bill at work, without comment. I went downstairs to cuddle my little girls.

When he came home that night, he had a defiant look on his face.

"Well, it's clear, isn't it?" he said.

"Is it?" I questioned.

"Of course, the super bitch stepmother has contacted Sofia's family, and he knows about the house now. He wants to get his mitts on his share, so he thinks he'll try and saber rattle a bit at the same time. I told you, all Sofia's family hate me with a passion. They all blame me for her death; you know all this already. Just forget about it."

"Is it true that you didn't tell him she'd died?"

"I couldn't tell him, I didn't have his contact details. They hardly knew each other anyway. I mean, they can't have been close; they barely saw one another. I tried to look for his address, but to be perfectly honest I had other things on my mind. My wife had just committed suicide and her leech family was crawling all over me trying to get their hands on whatever they could. Richard and I were never bosom buddies, and like I said, he and Sofia weren't close. I sent a couple of emails off, and when I got no reply, I left it at that, assuming he wasn't interested."

Of course, this didn't ring true to me. Nobody informs somebody of a death by email. There must have been more to it, but I decided not to push Bill for any more answers just yet. It was clear there was enough stress going on without us going over old ground again. I wasn't even sure I wanted to know anyway. I tried to put it out of my mind. I tried to put everything out of my mind. I wanted only to focus on the kids, but it was getting harder and harder. I'd started snapping at the girls. I'd been crying in front of them when we were alone during the day. I felt I was letting them down. I couldn't seem to think straight any more. My head was constantly pounding and I couldn't eat or sleep. What the hell was going on? How the hell had it come to this? What could we do to make things right again?

For our anniversary, I suggested to Bill that we have a romantic evening at home, with a nice meal and wine. I was hoping to put some spark back into our failing relationship. I had resolved that the stresses and strains we'd been forced to cope with since the beginning of our marriage had taken their toll, but we still loved each other, and I was determined to make it work. Bill cooked another of his amazing meals, and the evening started off well. But as the evening wore on, and the wine flowed, it once again loosened my tongue. As I sat there listening to Bill spouting his now predictable diatribe about how much bad luck he'd had, and how he always seemed to attract idiots, something inside me once again snapped.

"We've been married three years today," I said

"Yes, I know."

"It's been a hell of a three years, hasn't it?"

"It sure has." He wasn't smiling. He looked almost bored.

"Ask me if I'm happy."

"What?" He rolled his eyes to the ceiling in a 'oh here we go again' expression of exasperation.

"Ask me if I'm happy Bill. Do you think I'm happy? Do I look happy to you?"

"I'm trying my hardest to make you happy, but it seems at the moment nothing is good enough"

"Nothing's good enough? How can you say that after I've put up with so much in such a short space of time?"

"I know it's been hard, but none of it is my fault. You wanted to come to France, I didn't force you!"

"I wanted to come to France because thanks to you we were no longer able to stay in Switzerland full time. I wanted our family to be together, not thousands of miles apart. I had no choice but to come to France. But, Bill, it's your apathy that I cannot stand. I've never seen you pursue anything with such rigor and determination as you pursued me in the early days. Since we've been married, all that drive and determination has dissolved away! You don't look after yourself. You've gained weight. You don't want to take part in family activities. You lock yourself in your office. You say you are chasing 'big deals' but what deals? When has any single one of them ever succeeded? You ignore your youngest daughter! You have two daughters you know."

"I do not ignore Alice!"

"Yes you do! You don't even know you're doing it! It's not just me who has noticed it; my parents have noticed it too, they spoke to me about it when they were here, and again at Christmas."

"That's rubbish!" He said. "Listen, all you ever do is criticise me recently. You say I'm apathetic, but to be honest it's difficult to remain motivated when all you do it hound me. I need your support; I need you to believe in me! You say you want our relationship to work, yet how can it when we sleep in different rooms? We're not having a normal relationship. If we were having a normal relationship, I would be happy and motivated. As it is, you clearly don't like to be around me, so I keep out of the way. But know this, Sarah: I love you and I adore my girls. You are my world and I will do everything I can to give you the life you want. You just have to *really* want it, and you have to get back to believing in me."

"I want to believe in you, Bill, and I want our family to be together and happy. I'm just so scared and mixed up at the moment; it's been such a dreadful three years. I can't take much more of this! Things have to change. I want stability and security. I don't want controversy and arguments all the time. Please, Bill, I'm losing the plot!"

"Let me help you then, that's what I'm here for. You just have to trust me, Sarah."

"We can't stay here," I cried. "I'm going to go insane. Please, Bill, let's look for a house closer to the city."

"OK, we'll do that then, if it will help." He held his arms out to me. So I let him put his arms around me, and I tried to remember how it used to feel when he held me. I tried to remember what it was like to feel safe. I really wanted that feeling back, but no matter how hard I tried and willed it on, the feeling eluded me, and the sinking feeling in my stomach was all I was aware of.

The next day, the guilt was back. I felt terrible for the things I'd said to Bill last night. I didn't understand myself! Was I trying to push him away? And as the familiar guilt returned, so did the pattern of behaviour that accompanied it. For a while, I made a real effort to 'be a proper wife', and support Bill one hundred percent.

Two weeks later, Bill came home and said he'd seen a removals van outside his house.

"Good riddance," he'd said. "Let's get the damn thing sold now."

A few days later, we received registered post. It was from Bill's parents. I was with Bill when he went to collect the post. Inside the parcel, was the key to the house. A single key, taped onto a piece of card. On the card, Bill's stepmother had written one sentence:

'For what does it profit a man, that he gain the whole world, yet lose his own soul?'

Chapter Twelve

Attempts to Stay On Track

"We'll buy a house here," said Bill one day. "Would that make you feel happier? We can use the profit from the sale of the old house, and we'll get ourselves a lovely property within striking distance of the city."

This seemed like a logical thing to do now. We couldn't stay in the cottage; it was far too removed from Bill's place of work, and all my friends from the mother and baby group. I agreed it would make sense to finally putdown some roots, and put the last three years behind us. I wanted nothing more than to start afresh in a different place, away from the memories. At least when the house was sold, (I reasoned to myself) the whole Sofia chapter could be closed, and maybe we could move forward at last.

"Start looking for places right away," Bill had said. "If the house here hasn't sold, we can organise a bridging loan if we find something we really want. The main thing is, we can get away from this village and into a place that belongs to us."

I worried about how Bill was going to get a mortgage with his credit history.

"What the French banks don't know won't hurt them," he'd laughed. "All we have to do is provide the paperwork from our Swiss company. It shows how much money I've turned over since I went independent. I've taken advice; it will be enough to secure a mortgage."

And so, I began looking online for properties, and we handed in our notice on the cottage. I'd started to feel a bit better about things. I'd been spending more and more time with my new friends, and with their encouragement, I was starting to imagine a life in France. I was still missing Switzerland terribly, but I kept telling myself that I'd just have to let that go. If we were to stay together as a family, I had to focus on what was achievable. Bill remained confident that the contracts in the company would keep coming (with Tom's help), and he'd managed to secure a new contract in a department where he seemed to actually get on with the manager. He was still spending every spare minute on the computer. His latest 'project' was a website, which he was designing together with one of his new colleagues. Bill had always been a self-taught computer expert, but recently he'd been investing all his time in teaching himself to program entire websites. He'd surf the web every night, until the early hours, in order to teach himself the ins and outs of programming.

"The internet is the future," He'd enthused. "I'm going to build websites for people. It's simple, and the money that can be made is phenomenal."

"How does it all work?" I'd asked. "Easy, you can make money for doing nothing. It's all about the viral effect, you see. You attract people to your site, and they in turn bring more traffic. You can make money on click-throughs, advertising, sponsorship, anything is possible. We'll attract people to the site and charge them a small fee; they then get benefits when they bring their friends to the site. After the critical mass is reached it starts to roll all by itself. We'll make money in our sleep Sarah, just you watch!"

As usual he was utterly convinced, and as usual he put forward a very convincing argument. Despite still having reservations about everything that had happened to us in the last three years, I tried to believe in Bill. I kept telling myself he was going to make everything all right. I convinced myself to focus on our little family, and being the best wife and mother I possibly could.

That spring, we were invited to the fortieth birthday party of a friend of mine. It was to be in Gran Canaria. His partner had organised the accommodation at a knock down price, so I decided to ask Bill if we could afford to go. It would be our very first (and our only) family holiday. I hoped to use it as quality family time, and to try to get our relationship back on track. There was a large group in attendance on the holiday, and we were the only ones with kids. We didn't know any of the other people, apart from the couple who had organised the trip, but they were a friendly bunch and we soon got to know them all and enjoy their company. Once again though, I found myself cringing at Bill's behaviour towards Lucy, especially when he had an audience. He would sit her on his knee, and constantly attempt to get her to recite the alphabet, count to ten, or tell the group how many legs an octopus has.

124

Despite me quietly asking him not to show her off this way (she mostly refused to 'perform' anyway) he just ignored my request.

During the day, he would take Lucy in the pool, or for a walk, and as usual, Alice and I were left to our own devices. My birthday also fell during the trip, so we decided to hold a joint party at a local restaurant. In typical Bill style, he held court during the meal. He talked about his favourite subjects, boasted about his fantastic job, and repeated his usual repartee of unfunny jokes. As usual, I was acutely aware that several party members found him tiresome. It was written all over their faces. I was actually embarrassed on his behalf. This seemed to be happening with increasing regularity since I'd first become aware of it, at Bill's fiftieth birthday party. I wondered to myself if it had actually always been this way, yet I'd only seen Bill through rose-tinted glasses previously. I decided as usual to try to ignore it, and concentrate on having a good time. At the bar, my friend Ian caught up with Bill.

"So Bill, it's Sarah's fortieth in six years, right? Have you thought about how you'll celebrate it?"

"Sure Ian!" Bill had boasted. "I've been giving it lots of thought. Sarah always wanted to go to New York. I was going to take her there as part of our honeymoon trip, in fact, I'd booked it! Then 9/11 happened and I changed my mind. Now, I've decided to charter a jet and take her and a group of her best friends there. Of course, you're invited!"

And he slapped Ian on the back. Ian told me, much later, that he was really impressed. Chartering a private jet! Wow! He couldn't wait to tell his friends what Bill had said. Like many other people, he genuinely believed Bill when he spoke about his earning power. He put forward a very convincing argument. Ian said later that whilst he was slightly put off by Bill's brashness and bullishness, he was in no doubt that he was indeed the successful businessman he purported to be. Slowly but surely, over the next few months, my confidence in Bill started to creep back. He was so full of enthusiasm over his new internet project; it seemed this one really was going to be 'the big one.' Since beginning his internet journey, Bill was coming into contact with more and more 'like-minded' people.

"I've met two women who I'm going to go into business with," he'd enthused.

"I'm going to build fantastic websites for them both, and one of them has agreed to go into partnership with me! She's already quite well known in her field, and she has loads of contacts in the showbiz world. She can really open doors for me!"

It all sounded too good to be true, and I kept reminding Bill (much to his annoyance) that he still had to concentrate on the job he was actually being paid to do.

"You spend so much time on the computer," I said to him one day. "And I think it's great that you're so dedicated and determined to make this new venture work. I just worry about you. Lucy, Alice and I don't have much benefit at the moment. I'd like it if we could spend more time together. I know it's important that you do this work, and I really want this new project to be a success. But just remember you have a nine-to-five job, and you have two little girls here who are growing up so fast. Don't let this special time pass you by, please. "He nodded his head, as he always did. It didn't change things though: he was determined. As soon as he came home at night he was in his office, and he stayed there until the early hours of the morning, when he went to bed in the guest bedroom.

When I look back over this period now, with the benefit of hindsight, I often wonder what it was that motivated me during this phase of the marriage. It wasn't a deep love, at least not the one that I'd experienced in the first months and years of being wooed by Bill. It wasn't passion; there had never been any of that anyway. It may well have been loyalty. I had made a pledge to stay with this man for better or worse, and I took those vows very seriously indeed. I wanted so much for Bill to be the person I'd thought he was in the beginning. I didn't want to admit to myself that he might indeed be something or somebody entirely different. I deliberately blocked out the niggling voice that was constantly in the back of my mind. I was sinking into a sea of confusion, and at that time, it seemed to me as though Bill was the only thing I could hold on to. I honestly believe when I look back now, that the main reason I stayed with Bill, and continued with a relationship that I knew, deep down, was all wrong for me, was guilt. I was driven by

127

feelings of guilt, and a desperate feeling of inadequacy. To leave now would mean failure. I was the one who was failing, not Bill.

The feelings of guilt and inadequacy came all too often. Of course, I considered ending the marriage. Thoughts of breaking free were frequent, usually at night when I was lying alone in my bed. But they'd quickly be replaced by the guilt. I genuinely believed that many of the problems we were experiencing were down to my own shortcomings. I'd get angry and frustrated with Bill, and I'd let my feelings show. I'd be grumpy and ratty. I'd nag him and complain about things. He would then feel 'put down' and 'unappreciated', which in turn led to more self-reproach from my side. I'd often question him about his past, and this visibly frustrated him. To him, my questions showed that I didn't trust him. And without trust, he'd said, we had nothing. I had to trust him. I had to put my faith in him, or we'd never get out of this mess. If I wasn't standing by him, unquestioning and loyal, then I was exacerbating the situation for him, by undermining him. This in turn meant he was unable to 'solve the issues', and so the problem perpetuated itself.

I loved Bill, and I told him this as often as I could. But Bill loved me much more, so he said. According to Bill, I didn't (and still don't) know what love is. My feelings couldn't be compared to his, because they simply weren't as deep. It was Bill who had the monopoly on feelings, you see. I was always striving to match his depth of emotion. I felt unable to achieve the impossible goal he'd set for me in terms of 'exploring the depths' of our relationship. According to Bill, I'd never even attempted to 'scratch the surface' of our relationship. I thought I had. I thought I'd shown amazing patience and loyalty in the face of all the mishaps that had been thrown my way. I often wondered what more I could have done, how much more supportive I could have been. I honestly felt as though it was me who had failed, both as a wife and as a mother. I believed I had been wrong to complain, been wrong to show even the slightest doubt. I wanted to make things right, and the only way to do this would be to stand by him and devote myself to him completely. He was a better, more intelligent, more experienced, deeper, and a more empathic person than me. And until I 'understood' him and 'got onto his level' I was depriving us both of a potentially rich and fulfilling marriage.

I felt terribly guilty about this. I blamed his frustrations on myself. He was my husband, who adored me, yet I wasn't sleeping with him. He needed intimacy as a way of 'expressing his love', yet he wasn't getting intimacy from me. This was because Bill only wanted intimacy on his terms. There had been many times when we'd fallen into bed drunk, but this of course didn't count. There had also been a few occasions where I'd tried to show my love for him in a physical way, yet he'd been 'unable' to accept my attempted advances, as he'd said to me that 'I didn't really want it'. Actually, I had really wanted it, yet for some reason he had the impression I was only 'doing it for the sake of it' and so he'd politely turn me down; saying 'I'd rather never sleep with you again, than have you sleep with me out of a sense of duty'. At the end of the day, it was me who needed to improve. I did not have the intellectual capacity to understand our relationship the way Bill apparently did, and until I let him in, and let him guide me to this 'utopia' he always talked about, neither of us could be happy, and nor could our children. It was down to me, and I had to accept that. The solution was in my hands; of this I was convinced. I was at a loss as to what I should do for the best. So I tried to get things back to how they should be. I felt as though the ground under my feet was crumbling away by the day, so I searched for ways to cement myself to Bill and the girls. I focused on our family and let Bill focus on being 'the provider'.

* * *

During the autumn of that year, Bill had been asked to be best man at the wedding of one of his friends from Switzerland. The wedding was to take place in northern Italy, so we decided it would be a great opportunity to visit all our friends in Switzerland again. The wedding was a small affair, in a gorgeous setting. Bill was in his element, as he always was when he was to play a major role in an event. When we arrived, he introduced himself to everybody, sat down, and immediately began telling his usual repartee of jokes and stories. I was left to attend to the kids, and as we'd had a very long journey, I ended up taking them to bed, leaving Bill entertaining the wedding guests.

The next day, Bill was excited about performing his best man duties, and so I was happy to let him get on with it. I dressed the girls in their matching skirts and ponchos and followed Bill to the venue. The wedding followed the usual pattern of events we attended as a family. Bill was off, mingling amongst the guests and being everybody's best friend, and I was at the back taking care of the kids. When it came to taking the photos, Bill came and got the girls, so he could be photographed with one in each arm.

I was disappointed when it came to the meal. Bill was to be seated at the top table, and the girls and I were located at the very end table, next to the open door. I was more than a little disgruntled to be placed so far away with the girls, and whilst I understood it was for practical reasons, I just knew that I'd be left alone to look after the children for the entire rest of the day. And this was indeed the case. The only time Bill made any effort to come over was when he collected Lucy to take her to the top table with him and get her to perform the alphabet, or have her picture taken with him. I took the girls to bed when they got tired in the early evening, and we remained entirely alone until Bill rolled up in the early hours of the next morning. I was furious with him, but despite this I held my feelings back for the first time. It was the first occasion that I can remember where I'd really buried my own feelings, and bitten my tongue, for the sake of his. It was like I'd flicked a mute button inside myself, and with it I'd switched off a piece of my soul. This piece of my soul would remain silent for another two years, before it finally rose again, and saved my life.

Chapter Thirteen

Decision to Return

The day after the wedding, we drove to Switzerland. The closer we got, the more my anger from the previous night dissipated. I was exhausted, but driving up the familiar trunk road from Italy towards Southern Switzerland, I started to feel better. As we crossed the border, I felt as though I was coming home. Bill smiled at me when we stopped for refreshments just inside Switzerland.

"How do you feel?" he grinned at me.

"Honestly?" I replied. He nodded.

"I feel like we've come home; it feels right here. We've only been across the border five minutes, and already I feel like I want to stay forever."

"Well I'll tell you something honestly as well," he said. "I felt the same way you do!" I was amazed, and totally taken aback. Bill had always talked about his desire to settle in France. From the moment I'd met him he'd been very clear about it. I'd always believed that he'd never agree to us staying in Switzerland permanently. Hearing him say this was like music to my ears. I didn't think about the practicalities of it for one second. I just bathed in the knowledge that we both wanted to come back, and us both wanting it meant it was a real possibility. Suddenly, I believed I had the answer to all our problems. It was France that was making me so unhappy! It was the *place*, and not the situation we were in. That was it! If we returned to Switzerland, we could finally begin the life we'd always dreamed of. We could put the problems behind us, and settle down together in a place we both loved. It was the solution! Bill grinned at me,

"If it's what you want, Sarah, I'll make it happen. I'd do anything to make you happy, you know that."

"But what about work? We can't go back to you commuting again."

"It doesn't matter," he replied. "With my new projects and online ventures I can work from the moon! I don't need to be located in any particular place. I'll stay in the current job until we've sold the house, then I'll launch myself on the internet as a full time job, and work from home!"

Bill had an uncanny knack of pulling something out of the bag at times when he sensed I was at my lowest. He found ways of distracting me and making me feel better about things. He'd sensed my general frustration and he'd found a way to take my mind off it. He knew me well by now, and knew how I had a habit of fixing onto ideas. It had been the same when things had gone wrong in Switzerland, and he got me focused on moving to France. He knew I wanted nothing more than a steady and stable family life, and he knew that if he gave me something positive to focus on, things would improve between us. And they did.

133

* * *

Once the decision had been made, it was easy to get carried along with the excitement. My mind was constantly on Switzerland, buying a house there, and finally getting the life I'd been waiting for all this time. It seemed like a simple enough plan. We knew it couldn't happen immediately. The house needed to be sold first, and Bill needed to establish himself enough in his new project to enable him to leave the contracting job behind for good. We figured it would take nine to twelve months before we would be in a position to move back. In the meantime, we had handed in notice on our accommodation, so it was left to me to organise an interim solution. I was happy to be busy with organising things. It gave me a sense of purpose, and I didn't feel like a spare part just sitting at home all the time.

I found us an apartment in the city, close to all amenities. It was a temporary let, and fully furnished, so I arranged to have our furniture put into storage until we were ready to move it back to Switzerland. Leaving the isolated cottage and the village where Bill's parents had lived was a huge relief to me. I hadn't realised quite how miserable I'd become there until we left. The apartment was small compared to the cottage, yet I felt instantly at home there. I was within easy reach of my friends, and was surrounded by bustle and life. It was an amazing feeling. I relished being able to put Alice in the pushchair, with Lucy on the buggy board, and leave the house to walk to the local park and play on the swings.

When you've spent a year living in the middle of nowhere with two small babies and no facilities, being surrounded by city life and all it has to offer is like a breath of fresh air. The apartment had three bedrooms. The girls shared one, I had the main bedroom, and Bill slept in the small guest room. I was acutely aware that this was wrong, and that I needed to make an effort to change the situation, but I didn't know how to. We'd got into the habit of sleeping separately now, and it seemed like an impossible one to break. On the one hand, I knew I should be sleeping with him, but on the other, I was comfortable to let things continue as they were, because I was actually scared to try to change things. When we talked about it, we always went around in circles, with Bill insisting he was happy without intimacy, and preferred that to 'functional sex'. I would use wine to help me get the courage to talk to him about our sex life. I could never talk to him about it when completely sober. Indeed, I couldn't bring myself to sleep with my husband unless I was under the influence, and on the rare occasions when it did happen, it was always followed by a hangover.

Bill could drink. His dad had been an alcoholic, and whilst Bill seemed to me to be a long way off needing to go into rehabilitation, there was no doubt he was able to put away vast amounts of booze. I never understood how he did it. We'd share bottles of wine, and he never appeared to get drunk. He wouldn't get giggly or silly like I would, not unless he had an audience. When it was just the two of us, he always seemed to keep his cool. During our time in France, our alcohol consumption had been steadily increasing, to the point where by the time we moved to the apartment, the only really meaningful conversations we had were under the influence of drink. I often blamed myself for this. It must be me, I'd reasoned to myself. I can't talk to him without having had a drink first. This wasn't true of course. What was true was that the only way I could get him to talk to *me* would be if I got a drink into him first. He was so preoccupied with his internet projects, he clearly found the computer better company than me. It's possible I compounded the problem though, because when I had a drink, I either got silly, or I got deadly serious.

And whilst we lived in France, I became more and more preoccupied with Sofia. It didn't help matters that we were living close to where she'd died, and on one occasion Bill had pointed out their marital home as we drove past one day. Sofia became a distraction for me during this time. I found myself thinking about her more and more. I was starting to feel empathy for her and wanted to know more about the sort of person she had been. I kept telling myself to let it go, and not to bring it up, but for some reason I couldn't stop myself. There were things that I felt I needed to understand, and the only way I could understand them, would be if I could find out more about her; about what happened to her and why she did what she did.

"Why did you put the house in her name?"

"I told you, Sarah, because I wanted to show her I trusted her."

"But you said you were just business partners and friends; that's a hell of a gesture, isn't it?"

"So? What are you implying?"

"Well, maybe she thought there was more to it? Maybe she was in love with you?"

"Maybe she was. I always felt the relationship was more one-sided, but I never gave her any encouragement."

"But what about your kids' money? Didn't you check those bank accounts once in the whole ten years?"

"No, I told you I didn't. Why are you asking me about this?"

"Because I can't believe she could have been so dishonest for so long. She must have been very sure of herself, or of you! I mean, she was filtering all that money off right from the very beginning. You could have checked those bankbooks at any time and she would have been discovered. Seems she took a hell of a risk."

"So what Sarah, what is your point?"

"I don't have a point, I'm just trying to understand the woman and what motivated her to do what she did. Do you think her mother was an influence? She lives in a house paid for with your money, after all. Do you think she knew Sofia had ripped you off for all that money?"

"Probably. She was a nasty scheming old bag and she hated my guts. I don't know if she knew, but I wouldn't be surprised."

"But I just don't understand how you didn't know. Did you never check the accounts?"

"No, Sarah. The books were her responsibility. I trusted her. Can we drop this now please?"

"But I don't understand, I can't stop thinking about what she did. She was all alone in that farmhouse and she took rat poison. I feel sorry for her. I can't reconcile what you've said about the end of her life, with the person you've described to me, and the things you say she did. I just need to understand, Bill. Did you love her?"

"No, not in that way. I've told you, Sarah, and I don't see the point in going over this again and again."

"But you didn't trust her. You must have felt some distrust because you put all that money away on the Isle of Man, and you prevented her from selling your Porsche to make money."

With that, Bill banged his fist so hard on the coffee table that his wineglass fell over.

"ENOUGH!" He yelled at me for the first time ever.

"ENOUGH!! STOP BANGING ON ABOUT SOFIA... STOP THISNOW!!!"

I was stunned into silence. I'd never seen him so angry, and I'd certainly never seen him express his anger physically before. He'd never shouted at me either. This took my breath away because it wasn't the Bill I knew at all. He drew a deep breath, and then exhaled slowly. He regained his composure and then turned to me.

"We won't talk about this again," he said in a calm and monotone voice. "We've done it to death, Sarah; I won't keep going over all this shit. It ends now."

And end it did. I never spoke to him about Sofia again after that night. I didn't dare. I buried it for now, because I knew I needed to put it out of my mind for the sake of my marriage. It was quite clear from Bill's reaction that night that there would be no more discussion about this. I resolved to let it go, and made a conscious effort to do just that. I succeeded for a while, but over time it became apparent to me that I could never shut Sofia completely from my mind. My conscience would simply not allow it

* * *

Bill continued to busy himself with his internet projects. He was now in daily contact with two of his colleagues, one of whom was helping him to build a Joke website, which Bill was convinced was going to make 'millions', and the other of whom, had asked him to build a BDSM (Bondage and Discipline, Bondage and Submission) website. Bill was one hundred percent confident that both these websites, once launched, would require very little maintenance, yet reap enormous rewards, both for us, and the two colleagues who had provided the ideas and the material. The other 'major' project, was working with the UK-based women who specialised in relationship coaching. He spent a great deal of time talking to this woman on Skype (an internet communications tool), and together with her, he'd developed a concept for a whole series of websites (relating to her area of work) which were to be built and launched simultaneously, and which Bill was convinced would be 'enormous' and 'set us up for retirement'. Once again I hinted to Bill that it might be a good idea if he obtained some sort of legal agreement with this woman before spending much more time working with her, but once again I was dismissed. He seemed to think the upfront investment of his time and effort was a given, and that it would be rude to even think about asking this woman for payment for the hours and hours of work he was doing for her. So, once again, I bit my tongue.

Despite the good news about a return to Switzerland, physically and emotionally, I was starting to experience another dip. I was suffering from serious headaches, which painkillers were doing nothing to abate. I was also unable to eat, and sleep evaded me. I could feel myself sinking into a dark place again, similar to the feelings I experienced after Lucy had been born, but I didn't understand why I was feeling this way. I was trying to be positive and look forward to our exciting new life back in Switzerland, and the money that Bill's internet projects would surely reap. Why was I feeling this way? Why was wrong with me? I kept telling myself to snap out of it, but as time went by I knew there was no hiding from this 'thing' that was happening to me. I was snapping at the girls, my patience was very thin. I found myself yelling at them, then dissolving into a sobbing heap on the floor. Lucy would toddle over to me and put her arms around me.

"Don't cry, mummy," she'd say, and it would make me feel ten times worse. I lay awake at night with my mind racing ten to the dozen. I couldn't talk to Bill about how I was feeling, because I knew he wouldn't understand. I found myself putting on a brave face in social situations with my friends. I was becoming closer and closer to them, yet they knew a different Sarah, not the real Sarah. The woman they knew was happy and well adjusted. She had a great marriage and great kids. Her husband was a successful entrepreneur who adored her, and doted on his girls. They didn't see the real me, because I kept it very well hidden. I kept it hidden from them, and I kept it hidden from Bill. The people I couldn't hide it from were my girls. They saw the real me. They witnessed their mother turn from angel to demon. They saw me yelling and screaming. They saw me punching the wall and hurting myself, and then they saw me crying. They saw too much crying.

In the end I knew I had to do something before it got out of hand, so I made an appointment for Alice to see the doctor about a mild ailment she had, and whilst she was there, I mentioned to the doctor that I didn't think I was coping. That doctor was fantastic with me. She was the first person, apart from my mother, who really seemed to recognise that I had a problem. She immediately made another appointment for me to go back and see her the next evening after surgery had finished. I told Bill I had to go and see the Doctor, so he needed to look after the girls that evening. He didn't even ask me what the problem was, and to be honest I was happy about that, because I didn't really know what to tell him. I got the girls ready for bed, and left him sitting at the PC tapping away at the keyboard.

The Doctor asked me some basic questions about my life, and how I was coping with the kids etc. I didn't give her details at all. I merely said we'd had a difficult few years, and that the second pregnancy had taken its toll on me both emotionally and physically. I didn't attempt to explain anything else. I didn't need to. She heard my cry for help and she immediately referred me for counselling. She also prescribed Prozac, and a mild sedative to help me sleep. I came away from the appointment relieved, but at the same time confused. It had ever occurred to me before that I might be clinically depressed. Certainly the idea of taking antidepressants was scary, yet strangely appealing. I hoped they'd maybe take the edge of everything, and help me get a better perspective on my life again. Until I did that, after all, I'd never be able to salvage our marriage. And that was my primary concern.

When I returned home that night I found Bill at the computer, where I'd left him.

"So, what did the Doc say?" He asked.

"She was lovely with me. She's given me some medication," I replied, feeling very anxious about telling him what the problem actually was.

"What is it? Is it women's problems?"

"No, not as such," I replied. "She's prescribed me Prozac, and referred me to a therapist." Bill sneered.

"Really? Depression?"

"So she says." I hung my head down. "I suppose it's post natal, after all the problems I had with Alice and the pregnancy."

"Oh yeah, course, that'll be it," he replied. "Are you OK?"

"Well, no. Not really. I'm a bit confused, but I'm happy I went and asked for help."

"Yes, best you did," he answered.

"I had depression once you know," he said. "It was ages ago, when I was running the German company. My blood pressure had gone up, so the Doctor decided I was stressed. He tried to give me Prozac too, but of course I refused to take it. Told him I'd never take that crap. He made me go to the shrink too, or tried to," he laughed. " Sent me to some place with bloody soft music playing and jossticks burning. I never even made it through the door!" He raised one side of his mouth in a sneer.

"Bloody mumbo jumbo," he sneered again. "I could write psychology literature in my sleep. No way some jumped-up arse wipe was going to get me to lie on his couch. Still, it might work for you. Let's hope it gets you over this post natal depression....hey?" And with that he put his arms around me, and I wept.

Chapter Fourteen

Grasping On to Hope

The next few weeks saw me full of resolve once more. I was on the road to recovery (or so I thought) because I'd had the depression diagnosed and it was now being treated. I had so much to look forward to, with the move back to Switzerland and Bill's new-found internet success. Financially, things seemed to be looking up as well. We had almost paid back the wedding loan, and although money was always tight each month, I was at least comforted by the knowledge that we had no communal debts at that time. Of course, there was always a threat that the German bank would come back and try to get its money, but Bill was confident that so much time had now passed, they must surely have written it off. We were still registered as living in Switzerland, and we had maintained an address and an accountant there. Our taxes were being paid there, and on paper at least, the books looked healthy. All the accounts were in my name, apart from two accounts we had opened for the girls. They had a small payment each month, and we were intending to save up for them until they were eighteen. I had complete visibility of the accounts, as we did all our banking online. I rarely checked the bank statements though; it was mainly Bill's job to make sure all the monthly bills were paid. Sometimes I did wonder about why we were always living hand to mouth. We certainly didn't have the extravagant lifestyle we'd had before we were married. I was always careful to budget. I never bought expensive or unnecessary items, and I tried to keep our food budget to the bare essentials. We still seemed to struggle though, and for this I never had an explanation. Bill was earning good money throughout this entire period, and whilst we had the GE Capital Bank loan to pay off, it was still a puzzle that we didn't seem able to save. This worried me of course, but as usual, if I tried to talk to Bill about it he'd dismiss my concerns and remind me that within twelve months we'd never have to worry about such trivial nonsense again. His attitude to money was different to mine. We had a couple of credit cards (both in my name) and they were always maxed to the limit. He'd pay part of one off, and instead of thinking he'd lessened the debt, he'd think of it as having X amount *more* to spend that month, and immediately the available credit would be used on something else. It was a constant juggling game with money, and it made me very uncomfortable, but still I failed to tackle him about it, because I was always worried about offending him and upsetting the equilibrium in the relationship. As with most other things, I pushed it from my mind.

* * *

Just before Easter 2006, we received an offer on the house. It was for slightly less than we were hoping for, but it was a cash offer for a quick sale. We didn't need to think about it, we accepted immediately. We were finally going home! I was ecstatic!

146

"We need to celebrate this!" I said gleefully. "Let's book ourselves a last minute break! We can drive down to the med and find a little holiday apartment for the weekend, just the four of us!"

"Great idea!" said Bill. "I think we deserve a bit of a break. See what you can book."

So I found us a lovely little cottage in a small village close to the coast. We booked on the Wednesday, and we drove down on the Thursday for a long weekend. It was the first time we'd been away as a family since Gran Canaria, and the first time in months that Bill and I would spend time together in the absence of a computer. As was usual for us, we drank lots. Once the kids were in bed, Bill would cook and we'd open the wine. We'd spend the evening on the terrace, eating and drinking, and making plans for the return to Switzerland. I felt excited at the prospect of a new life; I felt confident that Bill had finally found a project which would reap financial rewards and bring us the security I'd longed for, and I felt satisfied that the problems of the past few years were finally fading away, never to return.

We slept in the same bed for the first time in about a year. It really felt like things were finally getting back on track for us. I started to regain some of the hope I'd had at the beginning of the relationship. I felt good about myself, and good about us as a family.

Contraception hadn't been an issue for us since Alice's birth. We simply hadn't been near each other. After the trip to the coast I wondered if we'd been a bit irresponsible, but when I actually thought about it, the idea of another baby didn't seem like a bad one at all. In fact, if ever the time was right, it was now.

"What do you think about having another baby?" I'd asked Bill after we returned from our weekend.

"Why, are you pregnant?" Bill asked hopefully. I could tell from the way his face lit up that there was nothing he'd like more.

"Well, I could be!" I replied. "It's not as though we were careful when we were away!"

"Well, I for one would be happy with the idea!" said Bill. "You know how much I love kids, Sarah; I'd be happy to keep on having them … a football team if I have my way!"

I wasn't pregnant from the trip, and I was surprised at how bitterly disappointed I was at this fact. We were back to sleeping in different beds again now, but relations had definitely improved, and now I was feeling so much better in myself (the medication had well and truly kicked in) I felt ready to give it another go, just to see what happened. I decided I'd just try the once, and leave it be if I didn't fall pregnant.

* * *

My therapist was a nice enough man, but when I look back now, he was just telling me things I needed to hear. This wasn't his fault. A therapist can only help you if you are honest with them about how you are really feeling. I wasn't being honest with him though. I wasn't deliberately lying to him either. I'd convinced myself by now that I was depressed because of having a problem pregnancy, then the move to France, followed by the isolation of living in the middle of nowhere. I fed my therapist lines about how I hoped for a better future in Switzerland, about my husband being an internet whizz who was building a fantastic business, which would enable him to work from home and spend much more time with me and the kids. The therapist didn't have much to work with, so he inevitably believed that the quick change around in my mental state was due to my change in circumstances, and that this would be all I would need to recover from the depression.

This was sealed when I fell pregnant the very next month. To me, and to my therapist and my doctor, this was the end to my problems. I was going home to start a new phase of my life, with my devoted husband by my side. It finally looked as though the problems were behind us, at long last. I set about trying to find us some temporary accommodation in Switzerland. We'd decided not to move back to the same place we'd lived previously. This was mainly because Bill felt he needed to be closer to Zürich and the airport, so he could travel for business, but there was also an element of not wanting to go back to the place where we were known, given the problems Bill had experienced with the company and the bankruptcy proceedings. We wanted to completely fresh start, in a familiar country, but away from the 'past' and all the problems we'd had.

* * *

It was a hot summer, but one full of hope and promise. As soon as I realised I was pregnant, I came off the anti-depressants. I didn't need the many more after all; what was there to be to be depressed about? I didn't notice much of a change when I came off them. Early pregnancy hormones were raging through my body as it was, so I put any extreme tiredness or confusion down to that. I was very focused during this time, focused and happy. I truly believed that things were turning around now, and that Bill and I could now put our problems away for good. Our relationship was still far from perfect, but I accepted that we were still in a transition phase ,and that things would settle down for good once we were 'home' and the internet websites he was currently working on were launched.

His relationship with his employer was once again strained, and it seemed even Tom wasn't able to smooth the path for him this time.

"Work's running out," he'd said to me. "It's a good job I've got my new venture, because the company is really struggling. They need to streamline, and that means no more consultants. I'm glad, because I can't work with this bunch of idiots any more. I'm sick of them not listening to what I have to say. They're a bunch of losers and I can do so much better without them."

"Just make sure you negotiate some sort of an overlap with them though," I'd warned. "Don't burn your bridges. We need income until the websites are making money, and you don't know when that will be."

"Don't worry, Sarah," he'd assured me. "They cannot finish this current project without my expertise. I have already told them that I will be leaving, and that I will complete the work from home in Switzerland and charge them a standard rate. They have no choice but to agree, because without me the project will fail, and money will be lost. Be assured, it's all in hand, I promise."

I felt that Tom had a lot to do with this. I didn't really believe the company would normally allow consultants to finish off projects from home, no matter how important they were. Still, it was a relief to know that everything was in place for our return, and that we would have an income for the interim period.

Alongside his day job, Bill now had three internet projects on the go. The one that was closest to completion was the Joke site he was working on with a colleague. The concept seemed simple enough. Members would sign up to the site, and rate each other's jokes. Each week, a small financial reward would be offered for the best joke, this money would come from membership fees. Bill was convinced we were going to 'clean up' with this project.

"Think about it Sarah," he'd said. "Millions of people go online everyday looking for jokes. All we need to do is get them to sign up to our site. We'll offer a free service at first, but encourage people to invite friends. It will soon go viral, and we can expect traffic in the hundreds of thousands each day. If we build up a membership of several hundred thousand, and they all pay four dollars a month each, can you imagine how much money we're going to make Sarah?"

It all sounded extremely appealing and plausible, and I couldn't help but share Bill's excitement about the launch of the Joke site, and about the other projects he was working on. The BDSM website was also starting to take shape. I couldn't quite believe that Bill was actually building a site like this, especially as he'd shown me some of the material they were using, which actually turned my stomach.

"But it's the business I'm in Sarah," he'd reassured me. "I'm an artist and a technician. I'm building spectacular websites for people. As far as I'm concerned, the content of the site is irrelevant. It all adds to my portfolio. As long as it's nothing illegal I'm not concerned. There's a huge market for this sort of thing, and as long as people pay money to view it, I'll build the site!"

I had to agree, it was a means to an end I suppose. And as he'd pointed out to me, it made business sense to get into an industry that generated millions every day. Sex sells, after all.

The third project was the one he was working on with the relationship coach in the UK. He was still spending vast amounts of time on this, and this was the one that tended to bug me the most. The other two projects were with people he knew and worked with, yet the woman in the UK wasn't a friend of his (or at least she hadn't been until recently). He was building a website for her for free, with the only 'deal' they had being a 'gentleman's agreement' that he would take a share of the profit once it went live. I really couldn't see the sense in investing time on something that guaranteed no return, if it wasn't a favour for a friend. It riled me, but as usual, I didn't say anything to Bill. I trusted him to know what he was doing.

Things moved quickly over the next few months. We exchanged contracts on the house, Sofia's relatives were paid their share, and we headed back to Switzerland with our share of the profit from the sale in the bank. I'd arranged for us to move into a house that would be vacant for twelvemonths. This gave us the opportunity to look around and find ourselves house to buy. It was an amazing feeling to be back. I felt unbelievably happy upon our return. The house was fantastic, and the neighbours were friendly. I was back in a country where I spoke the language. The pregnancy was progressing well, and Bill and I were getting on. It was almost perfect.

One of the first things we did was to make an appointment at the bank to discuss a possible mortgage. I was incredibly nervous about the meeting, as I knew it was inevitable that Bill's financial history would be brought up, and I couldn't see how it was possible that they'd lend him money for a house. Bill was confident as usual though, he didn't doubt his own ability to convince the bank manager of his success and reliability. And convince them he did. My account had one hundred and fifty thousand Swiss francs in it at the time we had the meeting about a mortgage, and Bill brought the accounts from the last three years with him, which showed a turnover in the region of one hundred and fifty thousand francs per year. It all seemed very healthy indeed.

"We'll be looking for a house in the region of one-point-two to one-point-three million francs," Bill had stated. "My current income is from Consulting, but the future income will be from internet businesses which I will run from my home."

He then proceeded to describe, in finite detail, the ideas he had for the Joke site, the BDSM site, and the 'Open the Doors' sites (the series of sites he was planning on building with the Relationship Counsellor). He illustrated his dialogue by drawing on the Bank Managers own note pad. He engaged the Bank Manager and the Financial Advisor of the bank in conversation about web traffic, BDSM, Google, and the Oprah Winfrey empire (which he said he was planning to emulate with 'Open the Doors'). He barely let the men get a word in edgeways, as he drew them in with his rhetoric and repartee. It was wholly entertaining to listen to, and it was incredibly engaging. He was a master at work, and there was no doubt by the end of it, that he was going to be able to get a sizeable mortgage from these men. To be honest, I've never seen anything like it before or since. I was amazed to see him in action like this. And to think I was worried he wouldn't get them to lend him money! There was no way they could have turned him down. By the end of the session they were practically begging him to use their bank for all his future financial dealings. They were eating out of his hand.

Then came the part where he needed to tell the bank about the bankruptcy. They were going to find out the moment they checked their computer files, so I nudged Bill under the table to get him to tell them upfront.

"There is a little something I do feel I need to mention now," Bill said to them.

"I've had a few difficulties in the past, through no fault of my own, but it means I now have a black mark against me, which is why the company and accounts are in my wife's name."

They looked at him inquisitively.

"I had a company when I lived in Germany. It was very successful and my late wife was my accountant. Towards the end of the time the company was in operation. I had a small cash-flow problem. A couple of my suppliers were on a ninety-day payment term, but of course I had to pay my contractors monthly. I approached the bank one month to get a bridging loan so I could pay the workers. They granted the loan, but then the supplier didn't pay me. They ended the contract without warning because one of my contractors had apparently breached their Data Protection rules. I was left high and dry, and ended up having to wind up the company very quickly. The money was never paid, and I couldn't afford the court costs to retrieve it. The rogue contractor fled the country, and I was unable to repay the bridging loan."

I froze in my seat. What the hell was he on about? Bridging loan? Rogue Contractor? Legal action against his German company? This was all totally new to me! Was he making this up? Why on earth would he say this? Why the hell didn't he just tell them the truth? That his wife had gone behind his back and taken out a massive loan in his name to pay for a house for her mother?

The Bank manager and his colleague nodded their heads and made sympathetic noises. Clearly they had bought the story, and it wasn't going to affect our chances of getting the mortgage.

"It's OK Mr Tate," they said. "These things happen in business. We can see from your books that you're financially fluid now. That's all we need to know. It won't be a problem." And with that they winked at Bill, and he winked back; a proper little gentleman's club. I was astounded. I was glued to my seat. What had I just heard? Had he made that story up to convince the bank managers? If so, he was a damn good liar. Or had he made up the story of the loan taken out by Sofia for my benefit? Either way, he was a damn good liar.

"A damn good liar."

The words reverberated around my head, over and over. The baby kicked me hard in the stomach.

Chapter Fifteen

Opening My Eyes

When we came out of the meeting Bill smiled at me.

"That went well!" He grinned. "I think we can safely say we've got the green light! Now all we have to do is find a house! Jeez, I feel great, Sarah; life is good! We've one hundred and fifty grand in the bank, I've got these new projects on the go, we're back in Switzerland, and we've got another baby on the way! Things couldn't be better!"

I smiled back at him, still wondering what it was I'd just witnessed back at the bank. Wasn't he even going to mention it to me? I was expecting him to say something like 'I'm glad they bought my story,' but he didn't .He just ignored it. Perhaps he thought I would bring it up? I sat in the car wondering if I should mention it, but for some odd reason, I just couldn't bring myself to do it. I couldn't face bursting the bubble and spoiling the congenial atmosphere. So, once again, I tried to put it out of my mind, or at least to the back of my mind. I wanted to enjoy the moment as well, and so I resigned myself as I so often did these days, to looking forward and not back.

* * *

Once we'd had the go-ahead from the bank, the house hunting began in earnest. We viewed several properties, and it was great fun to be finally looking for a place for us all to settle down in.

It wasn't long before I came across an advertisement for a new building development close to the Lake, with good motorway connections to Zürich. The location was about halfway between Zürich and the place we used to live, so it was within striking distance of both. We made an appointment to meet the salesman on the building site so he could show us around. It looked perfect, from what we could see. The salesman talked us through the plans, and showed us computer graphics of what the interior of the house would look like. It was a perfect size, with a bedroom for everybody, and had great access to local amenities. It was facing the lake, with spectacular views. Fully glass-fronted, with a decked balcony. It was pretty much everything I'd ever dreamed of. I'd never imagined I would be able to buy a brand new house, and choose all the fixtures and fittings! It seemed too good to be true, and of course I was worried about the financing.

"It's a lot, Bill," I'd said whilst we were still on site.

"It's do-able!" He'd replied. "We need a twenty percent deposit; that's pretty much exactly what we've got in the bank at the moment. But, we don't have to pay the entire deposit now. We can pay, say, fifty grand now, and the remainder of the deposit needs to be paid just three months before completion. The date for completion is next November, which gives us a grace period of twelve months.

158

By then the projects will be live and online, and earning money. The monthly mortgage repayment is no more that we are paying in rent now; in fact, it's slightly less. So, really it's a no-brainer sweetheart. I say we go for it. This is a fantastic opportunity, and we shouldn't let it pass us by!"

I agreed the house was amazing, and I could certainly see his reasoning over the monthly repayments. I had reservations about committing to such a huge deposit, but when Bill explained about the twelve month window, it did seem as though that amount of time would enable him to be well established with the 'Open the Doors' and other web projects. The figures he'd presented to the bank manager regarding those projects had been compelling. And I figured if he only made fifty percent of his predicted turnover, we'd still be able to afford the house comfortably. So I agreed. I signed the contract for the house, and we transferred fifty thousand into the account of the building company.

In the meantime, Bill was working flat out on 'Open the Doors' and the BDSM website. He'd given up on the Joke Awards site, declaring the colleague he'd worked with in that project a 'moron'.

"But you spent all that time working on it. It doesn't seem fair to me that you do all this work for nothing!" I'd nagged him.

"Sarah, I know, but put it down to experience. I really thought the guy had a great idea, and I built him the website exactly as he'd wanted it. The problem was he was unwilling to run the site the way I suggested. I told him if he went the way he was planning; it would flop. And now it's flopped, and he's blaming me! The guy's an idiot, and I'm not going to waste any more time on him. It hasn't all been for nothing, I've developed my skills and knowledge whilst working with him, and he introduced me to the relationship coach, Claudia, so in many ways it's been worth it. Don't worry. 'Open the Doors' is going to be absolutely massive. Claudia and I have been discussing expanding the number of sites from seven to fourteen. I'm going to have enough work to last a couple of years. And with the first sites due to go live in January, our income for next year is already guaranteed."

"That's fantastic!" I'd said. "I'm so pleased it's all finally coming together with Claudia. What about the contract though? You're supposed to be finishing that this month aren't you? Have you done it yet?" He shook his head.

"I haven't had time, Sarah! I've been too busy with the web projects."

"What? You've not done it? But Bill, they've paid you to finish it! You can't just leave it open like that! They'll never have you back!"

"Oh Jesus, Sarah, I knew you'd get all cranky if I told you. Just let it go please. I'll finish it. I won't let them down. The job will be done by Christmas, and done well."

I felt uneasy. This was typical Bill and so frustrating! Just because he'd lined up the next venture, he was failing to complete the last one! After everything that the company, and especially Tom, had done for us, the least Bill could do was see the job through to its completion. Now we were in Switzerland, and the company in France had paid him to complete work, which he hadn't done! It drove me mad that he had this lackadaisical attitude, especially as he proclaimed himself to be a professional expert and top class consultant. He'd bragged to a friend in France that he 'wouldn't get out of bed for less than a grand a day' and now here he was, taking money from a multinational company yet failing to complete the work package! From where I was sitting, he wouldn't be able to command that salary in a month of Sundays, not if his current form was anything to go by. Still, I realised there would be no point nagging, because the more I nagged him about it, the less likely he would be to do it. He'd leave the work deliberately to annoy me. Such was his nature.

December came around and I was really looking forward to Christmas back in Switzerland. I'd joined an international mums and kids group, and was really enjoying making new friends and getting into a new routine. I'd enrolled the girls in a private bi-lingual Montessori Kindergarten. They went two days a week, and whilst they'd been very reluctant at first, they were now settling in and had started to pick up the German language.

I was busy nesting. The last scan had confirmed we had a boy bump, and I was really excited about the prospect of having a son to add to the family. It was an adjustment to have Bill at home for most of the time. He'd set up his office in the basement of the house we were renting, and whilst he spent most of his time there, he would always have the door open and he'd allow the kids to roam in and out. They loved having him around, but he let them into the office with him whenever they wanted, which meant that during the times they were at home, he got very little work done. This meant that as soon as they'd gone to bed, he would go into his office and work until the early hours of the morning.

The house had four bedrooms. The girls had a room each, I had the master bedroom, and as Bill was 'working' such late hours, he would retire to the guest bedroom (in the attic), so as not to disturb me. This also worked in reverse, as he'd inevitably need to sleep longer in the mornings. The routine was working well though, until mid-December, when I started to get the dreaded, yet all too familiar twinges in my stomach. I was almost twenty-eight weeks pregnant.

I didn't hesitate in going to the Doctor's this time, and she immediately gave me strict instructions to stay off my feet as much as possible. She also prescribed medication to prevent contractions. It was pretty damn hard to stay off my feet with two little girls aged just three and two to look after, and I was grateful that Bill was around to help out around the house. He took over all cooking, shopping, and driving duties, whilst I was forced to stay home and rest as much as I could. Bill revelled in his newfound role of homemaker, which was absolutely lovely to see, except I couldn't help but worry about the amount of 'work' he was doing. Our income from the French company would cease this month, and until he had the websites up and running, there would be no external source of income. This would mean we would have to start eating into the one hundred thousand francs that was supposed to be the investment in the house. I didn't want to eat into this money. As far as I was concerned, it was already spent. We'd committed that money to the new house, and whilst we didn't actually have to part with it for another ten months or so, for each month we eroded those savings, we were living on borrowed cash. Bill didn't see it like me though. Bill saw one hundred thousand francs sitting in a bank account to which he had access. His perception was of a vast sum of money, at his disposal. We were financially sound, so why worry about how long it took for the money from the websites to come in? As far as Bill was concerned, once the money from the websites started to come in, we'd have so much money, we wouldn't know where to spend it first.

I saw this attitude displayed in all its glory on the day we went to the kitchen show room, to choose the fixtures and fittings for the new house. We'd dropped the kids off at kindergarten and made our way to the 9am appointment. The salesman must have thought all his birthdays and Christmases had come at once when he met Bill. Charming and eloquent as ever, Bill spent the best part of an hour impressing the salesman with his internet know-how, and telling him to watch out for the next big series of websites to hit the web. He detailed his BDSM project (much to my horror) and then presented a perfect sales pitch of the 'Open the Doors' concept. By the end, as with the Bank Managers a month previously, the Kitchen Salesman felt deeply honoured to be in the presence of such a genius, and would have moved heaven and earth to sell him his ideal kitchen.

"The kitchen is my domain," Bill had smiled at the salesman. "My wife prepares food for the kids. But I *cook*."

I smiled inwardly. I'd long since given up on cooking. I could never do it as well as Bill. He made even the simplest meal turn into a gourmet presentation, and he really did put all my efforts to shame. On the rare occasions I did cook, he'd either stand over my shoulder watching and commenting, or he'd just leave me to it. This would send my confidence crashing, in the knowledge I could never prepare anything decent anyway, and the only reason he'd eat it would be out of sympathy for me. The kitchen really was his domain, and I accepted that.

"The worktops have to be solid granite, several inches thick."

The salesman's eyes lit up.

"Certainly Mr Tate. I'll arrange that straight away!"

"And the sink needs to be right, as does the disposal unit. I must have an integrated disposal unit in my work area. And I need lots of light. I want light overhead and also integrated into the units. I need maximum light to work. I also need a food station. It has to be big, the biggest you have."

"Absolutely Mr Tate! Here's the catalogue for you to choose from!"

"And the storage needs to be just so. No wasted space. I want segments for all my utensils, spice racks and optimal food storage space. There must be ample work surface, and I want spaces for appliances such as kettle and toaster to be integrated into the cupboard spaces."

"Of course, Sir, and what about cooking facilities?"

"The hob has to be induction, and I need five rings. I also want a double oven, integrated microwave and separate grill facilities, please."

"Yes, Sir, that could work with the available space."

"We need to have a seating area. I want a breakfast bar with lighting."

"That might be a problem given the space," said the salesmen.

"Let's have a look at the plans then!" said Bill. He got the plans and poured over them for several minutes with the Salesman. I sat quietly in my chair, breathing through contractions.

"We'll re-design this part of the kitchen." He took a pen and started drawing on the plans. The Salesman was nodding his head (and no doubt rubbing his hands together). Once he'd re-designed the kitchen, the final item to choose was the overhead extractor fan.

"Actually, I was at a convention the other week and I saw something you might like Mr Tate," said the salesman. He disappeared briefly then returned with a brochure. He pointed to a piece of equipment that looked more like a top of the range flat LCD TV screen than an extractor fan.

"It's one hundred percent touch technology!" enthused the salesman.

"It's brand new on the market, not even on sale until next year!" Bill looked at the picture and smiled.

"Oh yes" He said, "That I just *have* to have. Where do you want me to sign?" And with that, it was lunchtime, and we'd signed our names to (what I perceived as) the most expensive kitchen in Central Switzerland.

* * *

Christmas was fast approaching, and so was the new deadline for Bill to complete his work package. I was still having strong Braxton Hicks contractions, but the medication was working and the Doctors were confident the baby would stay put as long as I took things easy. I was being closely monitored, but was thankfully able to stay at home. It was difficult to relax though. I was acutely aware that Bill needed to be in his office working, but as I was unable to tend to many of the household duties, he was left with the work load. I felt guilty about this, because he seemed to spend all his time looking after us, and very little time doing his paid work. He was still sitting up night after night until the small hours, yet when I questioned him about his progress he rarely had any to report. He was now fixed on the BDSM website, and had informed me it would be ready for launch sometime in the New Year.

"But you will have the work package completed by then, won't you?"

"Sarah, it'll get done when it gets done!"

I lost sleep over this work package. You can't just take money off somebody for a job and then not do it, and we really needed the final payment by the end of that month, or we'd have to start eating into the deposit money (which had already shrunk because of the cost of the kitchen). Just before Christmas, Bill told me he'd pushed the deadline for the work package out until the end of January.

"What did they say?" I asked.

"They weren't happy. But it's tough tits. Something had to give, so I decided it would be that."

"Brilliant," I sighed. "I guess you've burned your bridges with them as well now then?"

"Yes, I guess I have," he replied sarcastically. And I knew there would be no point discussing it further. I tried to plan a frugal Christmas, but I was off my feet for most of the time, and unable to do much in the way of present shopping. Bill was left to shop for many of the girls' gifts. I think they had the best Christmas ever, as their sacks were absolutely full to the brim of toys and other assorted treats. We had one hundred thousand in the bank, so Bill had spared no expense. That year he played Santa, and his adoring girls thought he was the best daddy on the planet.

* * *

By mid-January, the BDSM website was ready for its big launch. Bill had put in what seemed like hundreds of hours of work to get it all set up, and had so far received no money. He was expecting big returns quickly, but knew he had to market it properly. His partner in the venture transferred some money for the advertising costs. Bill duly switched the site to live, and used our credit card to place sponsored search engine advertisements on the web. We waited for the traffic to flow into the site and the money to come rolling in. It didn't. In the first week there were a couple of hundred visitors, and only one signed up.

"It'll just take a while to gain momentum," Bill had assured me. "Nothing happens overnight, just let it roll." I was starting to get really panicky now. Our rent for this month had come out of the savings account, as had the lease payment on the new and bigger car we'd just taken delivery of. All our living expenses would be coming out of the savings from now on, which meant to me that each month we would be a month further into debt. As we got closer to the September deadline, we would lose more and more ground. I

168

couldn't bear the thought of falling into a deficit with the house money. We needed the deposit money intact. Where was Bill's sense of urgency? He had no concrete idea when the new website would start to generate cash. He had no fixed launch date for the 'Open the Doors' project, and he had now missed two deadlines on the work package from France. I knew I needed to keep my stress levels down, for the sake of the baby, but it was getting increasingly difficult.

By the second week in February I'd had three false alarms, and was getting to the end of my tether. I tried very hard to focus on the baby and the girls, and not to nag Bill about his work. He was back to spending every waking hour in the office, and as I was so exhausted these days, I'd taken to going to bed almost as soon as the girls did, knowing I'd be up most of the night anyway, as night time was when the Braxton Hicks contractions would be at their strongest.

I was in a catch twenty-two situation though. How on earth could I relax when my husband couldn't tell me when the next pay packet was likely to arrive? I tried not to nag him, but his silence and unwillingness to talk about it just made me more uptight. It seemed the BDSM site had now faded into nothing, and the new 'Open the Doors' websites were still in the planning stages, despite Bill having supposedly spent hundreds of man hours preparing them. I really had no overview as to what Bill was doing down in that office day in day out, but whatever it was, it didn't look like it was going to generate an income any time soon. I was driving myself crazy with worry, and the worry was in turn resulting in more and more painful contractions.

Three weeks before the baby was due, the doctor decided to induce.

"We'll give you some more medication to get you through the next few days, and then we'll induce you at exactly thirty-eight weeks. He may well come on his own before then, but we'll try our best to get him through until next week," she'd said to me as I lay in tears in the hospital bed.

I didn't know how much more of this I could take. The last few days of the pregnancy were sheer hell. I was having hefty yet unproductive contractions constantly, day and night. I slept only in fits and starts, between contractions. I wanted it to be over. I wanted to get the baby out and get home so that Bill could finally get some work done. Once again, I felt responsible for our situation. As though somehow if I were not so useless at being pregnant, he wouldn't have to take timeout from work to take care of the girls and the house, and we wouldn't be in this scary situation. As usual, I transferred huge amounts of blame for everything back onto my own shoulders, which in turn compounded the physical and emotional problems I was having.

Thankfully, at thirty-eight weeks exactly, they took me into hospital to induce labour. On the drive in, we were both tense.

"Bill, this is driving me nuts. You know it is."

"Yes, I know Sarah, you've been telling me repeatedly."

"You've still not finished the work package."

"You know I haven't had time Sarah."

"But what about Claudia, can't you get her to sub you? Surely she should pay you for all these hours you've invested into her project?"

He shook his head and drew his breath.

"Please Bill. I'm scared! We'll lose the house if you don't start earning again soon!"

He gripped the steering wheel hard, then turned, and for the first time ever, spoke to me with disdain in his voice.

"Sarah. Let me worry about the money. Don't worry your pretty little head about it. Focus on the kids. *That's* your job."

And with that, I choked back more tears as we headed into the hospital to deliver our third child.

Chapter Sixteen

Light, and Then Dark

About nine hours later, after a long and unexpectedly difficult labour, Tim, my gorgeous little boy, was born. Bill had been at my side throughout the day. He'd entertained the midwives and the obstetrician with his usual dry humour and charm. He loved to play the doting husband: mopping my brow and tending to my every need. The hospital staff clearly thought I was a lucky lady indeed, to have such a loving and attentive partner.

I put my worries and reservations behind me for a few hours, to concentrate on getting Tim safely into the world. The first hour of Tim's life was a life changing experience for me. After the midwife placed him on my tummy, I left him there and let him find his own way up my body. He was incredible. Little by little, he inched his way up until he found the breast, where he latched on of his own accord. It was such an amazing bonding experience, one that will stay with me forever.

Throughout my pregnancy with Tim, I'd often wondered if I could possibly love him as much as I loved the girls, because he was the third, and because of the circumstances into which we were bringing him. This couldn't have been further from the truth, though. He was my little star from the moment he was born, and just like with the girls, I was overcome with

172

love. Many people have wondered why I went ahead with a third pregnancy, given the situation I was living in. Nobody has questioned this more than I have, believe me.

Did I do it because I thought it might help the marriage? Yes, definitely. Was it wrong to do it for this reason? Perhaps, given the way it all turned out. It was certainly a misguided decision, without a doubt. Would I do things differently given the chance? No, certainly not. Tim and the girls became my saviours. Three innocent children, who did nothing wrong, and who didn't ask to be conceived. Those three children gave me strength, and continue to do so to this day. I'd never say I regretted any of them. While Tim was perhaps a product of my own self-deception, he's also the living proof of how badly I wanted my marriage to work. There is so much to regret about the decisions I made during this extraordinary period of my life. So many things I wish I'd done differently and so much reproach for staying with Bill as long as I did. But I could never regret my decision to have Tim. One look in his eyes is all I need, to reassure me that he was, without doubt, one of the best decisions I ever made.

From the moment we returned home from the hospital, life reverted to 'normal,' except now we had another little person in the household. Bill purported to be working closely with Claudia, despite being three months late on his deadline for the work package. He kept profusely assuring me that money would soon be rolling in from the 'Open the Doors' project. And indeed, he did seem to spend a great deal of time talking to Claudia via Skype. They were building an empire (or so I was told) and it was soon to be launched with much fanfare. I reasoned that he must be creating something magnificent, given the endless hours he spent interacting with this woman, and working on her websites.

Deep down I knew he was spending his time doing what he always did … nothing. I decided not to challenge him any more about the work package. It was clear even to me that the company would never offer him work again. He'd let them down, and shown himself to be completely unprofessional in the process. Not even Tom could salvage his reputation with them.

For me, the chinks in his armour were starting to jump out. I no longer swallowed his flowery (and extremely persuasive) rhetoric about why he hadn't been able to complete the work, that is was their fault for not providing this or that. But I saw no point in telling him I was starting to see through him. Instead, I did what I always did. Focused on the kids and ignored that voice from within and its increasingly urgent cry for me to take action, before it was too late.

Tim and I were having problems with feeding. Once again, I was in complete agony twenty-four/seven, and it was not only affecting Tim and me, but also Lucy and Alice.

The girls had adapted so well to having another baby around. I was amazed and full of pride at the speed with which they adjusted. But having a mummy who was constantly in agony, to the extent that I wasn't even able to hug them, began to take its toll on us all. My life became a blur of doctor's visits, midwife check-ups, household chores and kindergarten runs. Tim had terrible colic. He screamed almost non-stop and wouldn't let me put him down. It was horrible to see him so distressed, and it wasn't until several weeks after his birth that the midwife suggested cranial osteopathy. He'd been a 'back to back' baby, and had spent forty minutes stuck in the birth canal, with his head bent backwards as far as it would go. According to the Doctors, he'd suffered some stress injuries as a result, and they thought maybe cranial massage would help.

Luckily it did, after three or four sessions, and I hoped this would see the end of our health issues. Sadly this wasn't the case though. I was taking much longer to recover from the birth than expected, and I found my energy levels were unbelievably low. I had the familiar 'walking through treacle' feeling once again and I knew this was much more than just the average baby blues. It didn't help matters that I was being left to cope alone almost exclusively. I was partly to blame for this though, because I was so terrified about our ever-dwindling bank account, that I was reluctant to accept any help from Bill even when it was offered. I had hoped, though, that he might be able to resume some sort of normal working pattern, now I was once again available to look after the children full time.

We were still in separate bedrooms of course, so when I got up with the kids in the morning, he would stay in bed, only rising at about nine ready to resume his day of office work.

But his day never ended at five in the evening. He would surface for a short while, perhaps to help with the bath, to cook something to eat, but as soon as all the kids were in bed, he was back down the stairs into his office, and onto the internet to plan his world-wide-web takeover bid.

I was lonely; pure and simple. I felt desperate. I wanted to help, but didn't see how I could do any more than I already was. I wanted Bill to appreciate my efforts, but I felt he could only do that if I stopped nagging him about money. So I tried not to mention to him how concerned I was about our financial state. I'd given up checking the bank statements long ago, and now I gave up asking him how long we had before we hit the breadline. I knew I couldn't cope with the answer if I had heard it. I worried constantly about the house we'd committed to buy, with its fancy kitchen and view of the Alps. I lay awake worrying about the state of our relationship. I lay awake wondering what I could do to make Bill into the person he was when we met. I truly believed it was me who was the problem, despite the knowledge deep inside me that he was never really the person I thought he was. The Bill I'd met all those years ago didn't actually exist. I could see that now. The man in the basement was the real Bill. But had I turned him into that? Again, the doubts would creep in and eat away. I nagged him too much; I wore him down. I complained that he wasn't motivated enough, yet my very complaints were demoralising him even more. I didn't know what to do for the best.

I went to the Doctor; she diagnosed post-natal depression, and prescribed more anti-depressants. I fixated on the tablets. They were going to cure me and thus cure all our problems. If I could just cut him some slack, we'd be OK. I kept telling myself this, over and over. But it wasn't enough. He withdrew more and more, and inside I became more and more disconcerted. I started to drink, in the evening after the kids were down, I'd reach for the wine. I tried to engage Bill in conversation, get him to talk to me about our situation and maybe begin to plan a realistic way out. But invariably, he'd come and sit in the lounge with me, and inside ten minutes he'd be fast asleep. I would sit there looking at his reclined head and his open mouth, listening to him snoring loudly, and I'd sip my wine and wonder what the hell I ever saw in him.

This was the man who'd promised me the earth. So far he'd delivered nothing but grief, shame and misery to me. Were it not for the kids, I would have openly despised him. But kids make things different, they change your perspective, and they most certainly change your priorities. Your needs become secondary to theirs, and your own hopes become secondary, and almost irrelevant. I looked at him in one moment and felt bitterness, and in the next I'd feel sorrow and shame. For he was the father of my children, the man I'd pledged my life to, and to leave him now would be out of the question, wouldn't it?

By the beginning of May, when Tim was just two months old, I knew I needed to get my head sorted out, and I knew it wouldn't happen whilst I was under the same roof as Bill. I decided to get away with the kids, to the UK, and the sanctuary of my parents' home. I knew Bill would not oppose the trip. I knew he'd actually welcome it. With me and the kids away he had free reign to speak to Claudia and whomever else he wanted on the internet. The web was Bill's new home. He felt at his happiest online. His wife and kids were no longer uppermost in his mind.

I needed some time to think. By now I knew there was little chance we'd be able to buy the house. The kitchen fitters had already sent three demands for money that had gone unpaid. Despite Bill's repeated assurances for me not to worry, I knew he was never going to be able to pull anything from the hat. If he hadn't been able to do it in the last five years, he wasn't likely to be able to do it now.

I boarded the plane with a heavy heart. During the flight it occurred to me for the very first time that I might not even be going back. It would have been easy to make the decision once I was hundreds of miles away. The thought sent a rush of adrenalin throughout my entire body.

Could I leave him? Could I see the kids and myself going it alone? Did I have the strength? Suddenly, the whimsical thought began to take hold of me and become more solid. I spent the entire flight mulling it and over. Why not? I could do it, couldn't I? Get out now. Why not leave him to the mess he'd created. Why should I go back? I've taken enough by now, surely? I don't owe him anything, do I?

Then I looked at Lucy, Alice, and the sleeping Tim, and the feeling crumbled. It didn't dissolve though, far from it. The thought was planted in my mind now, and the roots were taking hold. If I didn't consciously fight the desire to leave him, it grew and grew like weeds in an unattended garden. In unchecked moments, I'd find myself drifting off, and daydreaming about being free. I fantasized about being free, just the kids and me, away from him. Free to start a new life.

* * *

The visit home was lovely. Never before had it felt so good to be there. I loved being in my mum and dad's house, and having them around to help with the kids. The kids adored the attention they got from their grandparents, and they certainly appreciated the difference being away from Switzerland made to me. We spent some lovely, stress-free moments together, just the four of us. I took the kids to the local park, or to feed the ducks, and we played and laughed, and did all the things normal families should do. It's amazing how responsive kids are. They are little sponges, they absorb everything, and this includes the negative as much as the positive. You might not notice when you're living under a cloud of stress, but they know it too, even at a very young age. The difference in the kids whilst we were in the UK on that visit was tangible. I knew it, and my parents knew it. I talked to my mum at length. I poured my heart out to her, whilst we both pretended to my dad that all was well. My mum and I had decided to keep Bill's past a secret from my dad, for Bill's sake really. We knew my dad would judge, and we didn't want that, so we decided it would be best to say nothing. My mum had been the only person I'd ever been able to talk to about this, until now.

I caught up with friends whilst I was in the UK, and inevitably the question arose as to why Bill wasn't accompanying us on this trip, given that he'd always made it clear to everybody we knew that he'd never let us all out of his sight for a second. One night, while I was out with a good friend and her partner, the floodgates within me finally opened. I mentioned to my friend that all was not well, and as I tried to explain the situation we were currently in, I found myself having to 'fill in the gaps' so to speak, and ended up relaying the entire background, from Sofia, to Bill's parents, to now.

My friends sat open-mouthed. They clearly could not believe what I was telling them. When I relayed the story, and heard the words coming out of my mouth for the first time (in one go), I really couldn't believe it myself.

"You are crazy!" My friend exclaimed.

"Sarah ....what the hell are you doing with this moron? Get the hell out now, while you've still got the chance!"

"I know, I know," I'd replied, half-heartedly.

"You cannot seriously think you can stay with this person! After everything he's put you through? He's a *loser*, Sarah! Get out now or you'll end up like Sofia!"

"I'll never end up like Sofia," I said. "I have the kids to think about, and her circumstances were different to mine anyway."

"And you're sure about that, are you? I mean, you actually believe him? He's lied to you, Sarah, about everything! He's certainly lied to you about Sofia!"

I knew she was right. I'd known it for a long time. He was a good liar, a 'damn good liar'. I remembered the day at the bank. My friend was furious on my behalf, and rightly so. If I'd been her I'd have reacted in exactly the same way. Yet, for some strange reason, I didn't find this conversation with her was helping me. On the contrary, bringing it out into the open like this was absolutely terrifying, and I felt myself instantly regretting telling her the details of my life. Maybe it was shame, because I knew how bad it must look to other people. I felt embarrassed and ashamed that I'd stayed with him. I felt I was being judged for making a poor decision. Suddenly I felt confused and derailed again. My newfound resolve to get the kids and myself away from Bill was suddenly dissolving. Hearing their words and seeing my friends' reaction, made it all suddenly very, very real. I wasn't ready to deal with reality. I wasn't strong enough. I was completely and utterly terrified. There seemed to be no way out, and no way back in either. I was completely thrown off balance and had no idea how to resolve the situation. It was very easy to dream about getting away, and it was certainly easy to get angry and fired up when sitting in an English pub, with my extremely infuriated friends for company. I did a quick reality check, though, and I instantly realised that actually doing something about this was not going to be as easy as it seemed here in the pub, with several pints of Guinness inside me.

I didn't sleep that night. Everything was playing over and over in my mind, and I couldn't switch it off. How could I just walk away? What the hell was I supposed to do? I had nothing to walk to! I had no job, no security, and three babies who needed nurturing. I felt utterly desperate. I kept reminding myself of my old feelings for Bill. I was glossing over all the bad stuff, and focusing only on the man I'd known in the beginning. It's difficult to describe how my thought processes were during this time, but all I can say is that I was literally grasping at straws. It's better to deal with the devil you know, than the devil you don't, or so they say.

"How could I leave?" I said to myself. "I'm nothing on my own. How would I cope?" And so it went on, and on, until the voice inside me started to say what I wanted to hear.

"OK, you can do this, you can make it work, but you have to make some changes."

I knew I had to get behind my husband, and take more of a frontal role, if we were to salvage this marriage.

"He's a talented man" I thought, "but he needs direction. Maybe if I get into the driver's seat with him, and work with him, we can achieve things *together*."

Of course!! This was the solution! Why had I missed it all this time? I'd been so busy 'letting him get on with it' I'd failed to see what was right under my nose! Bill needed me to be right *beside* him, not behind him keeping the home fires burning.

"That's it! That's how I can save the marriage!" I'd exclaimed to my mum, who looked forlorn.

"It's my company too! I'm the Managing Director on paper! I'll become active in the company! We can live and *work* together!"

And so I convinced myself that this was the way forward, and I spent the next few days racking my brains about what I could do to help my husband and me build a successful working partnership, and in turn salvage something from the wreck that was currently our marriage.

Chapter Seventeen

Silly, Silly Sarah

Many different options had been going around my mind. I had visions of becoming Bill's PA, and taking care of all the general administration, whilst he then had time to concentrate on creating the websites for Claudia. I then went on to fantasise about becoming a true business partnership, with me helping to negotiate contracts for Bill. I let this thought run away with me, and actually began to visualise us building our own series of websites, independent of anybody else. I started to develop a concept in my mind. What if I were to become the creative force behind the websites? I could work on a series of ideas and Bill could then design and build the websites. Maybe if we put our heads together, we could come up with something workable, and if I was involved creatively and practically, it would give Bill and me a new incentive to pull together. If we pulled together and helped each other on a business level, it stood to reason that our general relationship would improve as well. We'd have a common purpose, we could build something together, and we could finally become the family unit I'd always dreamed of and longed for.

I started thinking about the joke website and what had gone wrong with it. Bill had been so convinced it was a fantastic and workable idea, so why had it failed? By chance, my mother had been sorting through some old boxes whilst we were over visiting, and she'd found some old school books and papers from my childhood. Amongst the papers, were pages and pages of poetry I'd written. I'd always adored writing poetry as a child; it was one of my favourite ways of expressing myself. I'd written poems on all conceivable subjects, and my mum had saved the lot. Reading my innocent childhood musings, I started to wonder about poetry on the internet. It was bound to be hugely popular. I wondered if perhaps building a poetry website together would be a way to get Bill and me started in our joint venture.

"How about an Internet Poetry Award?" I sent a text to Bill from England.

"Great idea!" he replied. I called him.

"I was thinking we could turn it into a member driven site, just like the Joke Site. We could have a special, dedicated page for each member, somewhere for them to showcase their work. Other members could come and rate the poetry and ultimately we could encourage people to submit poems into a monthly competition, the same as with the joke awards. This would be a way of generating a small income."

"Yep, that could really work!" was the enthusiastic answer.

"And Bill, this will be the first in a series of websites. I want to work with you! We can build our own internet business, you and I! We can use the company that is already set up in our names. I had been thinking of getting back to work, and this seems like the perfect solution. I can work with you; we can build something. What do you say?"

"I say it's worth a go, Sarah. I'll start putting some thought into the poetry site. I'll try to come up with something by the time you get back from the UK. I'm still madly busy with Claudia, but I'll find time to do this as well. I think your idea is a good one!"

He seemed to like the idea of creating a poetry website, but I wasn't sure how he found the idea of us working together as a team. It was difficult to gauge his reaction over the phone. I'd just have to wait and see.

The journey back to Switzerland was one of mixed emotions. On the one hand, I was excited about the prospect of getting 'back to work' and helping Bill with his internet projects. I was resolved to get behind my husband one hundred percent, and to work with him to create something we could build on. I still had confidence in his abilities; there was no doubt in my mind that he was an incredibly talented man. I'd convinced myself that all the knocks he'd endured had only thrown him off balance, and that he needed help with direction. This is where I wanted to get involved. He had the talent; I would help to drive his various projects through to their conclusions.

On the other hand, though, I was filled with trepidation. It was now June, and we'd seen no income at all in over six months. Bill now had full overview of our finances. I hadn't checked the bank accounts in months, but I knew that we were seriously running out of time. I knew deep down that we would lose the house, but I needed to persuade Bill of this, and see if he could get us out of the contract without losing all the money we'd put in so far. Despite Bill's continued reassurances that all would be OK, I felt sick every time I thought about the house and our ever-decreasing pool of money. The house we were currently living in was only rented on a one year lease, which meant that by October, just four months from now, we needed to have found another home for our three children.

Upon our return from the UK, I managed to persuade Bill to sit down with me and discuss our options for the future. I explained to him my ideas for the websites, and how much I was determined to help him with his work, in whichever way I was able. He seemed OK about me working with him on a series of new websites. He really liked my idea for the poetry site and had already done a considerable amount of work on it. He was less enthusiastic about my suggestion that I work with him and Claudia on 'Open the Doors', or even that I get involved in any way with any of his other 'ventures'.

"You've got enough on your plate, Sarah," he said. "I think it's great that you want to help with some new ventures, and I think it's a great idea, but you must leave the projects which are currently running to me. We may confuse the issue otherwise."

That was fair enough, I reasoned, and I allowed myself to begin making mental plans for the series of websites we were to create together. I would go jogging every day, and always my head would be full of ideas and plans for our joint venture. I wanted to start with the poetry site because this was something I felt I could really be involved in, and really feel comfortable dealing with. I knew I had a talent for writing, and even though my confidence seemed to have taken such a kicking these past few years, I truly believed I could build something special with Bill's help, and give other amateur writers such as myself a site where they felt they belonged.

Once the poetry site was established and working, I wanted to duplicate the format of the site to build a whole series of sites, all along the same lines. I imagined a social networking site for women, a magazine site, a home-made news site, and a micro-blogging site, all with the same theme, and all run by myself and Bill. I really convinced myself that we could do it, and that if we worked together, we would finally be able to create the stability I'd always longed for.

The next few weeks were a blur. Bill still spent every waking moment in his office, either finishing the poetry site, or talking to Claudia about their empire. He had also made acquaintance with a couple of other 'like-minded' business men, and was beginning to talk about doing deals selling funds, brokering finance deals, and working with a company who was encouraging investors to put money into planting teak trees in the Southern hemisphere. All these things were keeping Bill busy, and all these things were giving him a reason to stay away from the children and me.

I tried to remain upbeat, and threw myself into helping Bill with the creative ideas for the poetry site, whilst maintaining house and home, and looking after the kids. I was fighting a losing battle though, because with each passing day, I was becoming more and more concerned about our future living situation. One day, I decided I simply had to broach the subject.

"Time's running out, Bill, you know that don't you?" He sighed.

"Yes, Sarah, I'm fully aware of that fact. Even I know what month it is. I know what needs to be done. I don't need you to keep reminding me, but thanks anyway."

"What's happening with 'Open the Doors'?"

"The same as last time you asked Sarah. Shall I repeat to you what I explained last time?"

"I'm asking because I'm seriously worried now, Bill. You don't seem to be bothered by the fact that if we don't pull out of the house contract soon, we will be in way over our heads! As much as it breaks my heart to say this, we have *no choice* but to withdraw from the contract, and try to get some money back, otherwise we stand to lose the fifty thousand we put down."

"Do you honestly think I'm not aware of this, Sarah? Do you seriously believe I need you to keep reminding me? I am working incredibly hard here, under enormous amounts of pressure and strain. Your repeated insistence on telling me

189

where I'm going wrong does little to help our situation. Putting added pressure on me isn't helpful! Just *back off* and let me sort things out my way!"

And so I tried to back off, and I tried to ignore the feelings of bitterness that were once again eating away in the pit of my stomach. This wasn't helpful, I kept telling myself. I needed to work with him and not against him. I needed to keep focused on the future, on the kids, on our family. I kept saying these things to myself, over and over. But the rot in my stomach was spreading, and my emotional state was becoming more fragile by the day.

* * *

In late July, we launched the poetry site, and to my amazement, Bill spent almost one thousand francs of our remaining money on advertising. I kept my dismay quiet again though, as I felt I had no reason to complain, as this was my website after all. The investment seemed to work though, as within a couple of weeks, we had a couple of hundred active members, and we'd received lots of positive feedback. Work was continuing on the house, and despite my pleas, Bill was still arranging for flooring and other fixtures and fittings to go ahead. Work on the hideously expensive kitchen had now been halted, however, as the kitchen company were awaiting the second non-forthcoming instalment.

By August, Bill had somehow managed to position himself between a local car showroom owner and a Russian financial consortium, which was looking to invest in Switzerland.

"I'm going to broker that deal I told you about months ago!" he enthused.

"What exactly is it all about?" I'd asked, sceptically.

"Well, basically Herr Braun is desperate for money to expand his business. He's secured a deal with a Russian four-by-four manufacturer, to import its product into Switzerland. He needs money to expand his premises and market the new product, but I really believe he's onto a good thing. The problem is his business plan; it's a load of rubbish, and he can't get any of the Swiss banks to touch him. My lawyer, James, has contacts with this Russian financial consortium, and he's agreed to put me in touch with them with the view of me brokering a deal between the two parties."

"Sounds good, but what's in it for us?"

"Hopefully between ten and fifteen percent of the deal, which could mean a payment in the region of one hundred and twenty thousand Swiss francs. Enough for us to still get the house!"

I looked at him, unable to share his excitement.

"Bill, either you get this sorted within the next month, or we pull out of the house deal. I won't even consider this unless you get a contract up front. You've been working for people for years, doing them favours without a contract. I agree this sounds promising. James is a serious man, and I've seen Herr Braun's business for myself. But please, get this man to sign something or we can't let the house deal go any further."

He sighed. He hated me offering my opinion in this way. But he reluctantly agreed to draw up a contract with Herr Braun, and fortunately, James the lawyer agreed to help. This gave me fresh hope.

* * *

The poetry site continued to grow, and whilst it wasn't generating any income whatsoever to cover the server costs, at least it was attracting a decent bunch of people who seemed to take great pleasure in what the site had to offer. Bill spent a great deal of time and effort making modifications to the site, taking on board both my ideas, and the suggestions of the members themselves. We quickly had a forum, and a chat room. There were a few core members, who came back day after day, and kept the place ticking over nicely. I was pleased with the way things were going, and I was enjoying being part of it all. It was a boost to my much-deflated confidence, to post my poems on my own site, and receive some critical acclaim for them.

During August, some friends of ours suggested coming up to see us one weekend. It was the first time we'd entertained properly since we'd been back in Switzerland, and we both decided it would be nice to forget the pressure for a weekend and enjoy the company of friends. Preparing for the visit, Bill reverted to his old and jolly self. He spent hours planning an elaborate five star menu to impress our guests, and even went so far as to order a bespoke table decoration from the local florist.

No expense was spared, as usual. Our guests arrived and the evening began in really good spirits. I was enjoying showing off the kids to my friends, and talking to them about their plans and activities. It wasn't until the evening wore on, and Bill started to talk about his work, and the new house, that I started to get really uncomfortable. He produced the glossy sales brochures from the house, including details of the kitchen on which the work was now frozen. He bragged about how the kids would have a room each, and what kind of flooring we'd have (even though the flooring people had also stopped work by this point). He then went on to enthuse about his various business ventures. About the BDSM website which was 'about to be the next big porn site on the web' (even though it had been launched back in January, but had yet to attract more than a handful of members). He spent what seemed like hours droning on about Claudia, and how she and he were to build an empire 'bigger than Oprah'. He continued by explaining how he was about to broker the car deal, and was 'branching out – no pun intended' into the tree business. Our friends looked outwardly impressed, but I could see my girlfriend shooting me questioning sideways glances. She told me later she'd been reading the expression on my face, and knew something was badly wrong.

The next morning, as the men were sleeping off their hangovers, I ventured to tell my friend something of the real situation we were in.

"It's unlikely we'll be able to hold on to that house," I'd explained. "He's not earned any money in months, and we're getting to the end of our savings. He's got all these great projects in the pipeline, but none of them look as though they're going to come to anything in the next couple of months. I keep telling him to pull out of the house purchase, but he won't listen to me. I want to trust him, but I need to be realistic. He's not the successful entrepreneur he wants you all to believe he is."

My friend was dismayed, but not surprised.

"We've had our doubts for ages, Sarah. Some of the things he says just don't add up! What are you going to do?" I shrugged my shoulders in my usual resigned way.

"I'm going to do what I always do, and hope for the best," was my reply. My friend looked forlorn. She must have wanted to come over to me and slap me. She clearly wished she could shake some sense into this apathetic and downtrodden Sarah. I suppose it's a bit like seeing one of your loved ones sinking into alcoholism. You can see they are on a slippery slope, and you want to do all you can to help them get their life back on track, but you are powerless to do anything about it, because as with all depressed, addicted, or mentally afflicted people, they generally have to acknowledge they have a problem, before they are able to accept they need help. The Sarah I was then wasn't ready or able to see the predicament she was in. She was clinging on to impossible hopes and dreams, and refusing to acknowledge the very nasty and unpleasant reality of life. She was grasping at straws, and clinging on to her babies, desperate to keep things together for their sakes. She was unable to see what was underneath her nose, and she was unable to accept the huge mistake she'd made. It must have been incredibly frustrating for my friends and family to observe what was happening at this time. They must have been so frustrated and angry with me. Yet I carried on. I kept closing my eyes and ignoring the truth.

* * *

Silly, silly Sarah. How incredibly stupid I was, and continued to be, for things were about to get much, much worse.

Chapter Eighteen

Depression, Deceit and Despair

Finally, in September, about three weeks before the balance was due on the deposit, Bill conceded defeat and called the construction company.

"Is there any chance at all of getting our money back? Surely we've left it far too late," I asked.

"Why? We haven't finalised. Why shouldn't we get the money back? They'll easily sell the place; it's no skin off their noses. Don't be such a pessimist. We'll get it back."

I didn't believe him. I couldn't understand why he thought he could mess people around like this, and they'd actually pay him his money back. But I hoped I was wrong. This left us with a dilemma regarding a place to live. I called the people whose house we were currently renting, and they agreed to let us extend the lease until the end of November. That left me with two months to sort out an alternative. I was panicking. Bill wasn't panicking though; he was far too busy on my poetry website. Night and day, day and night; he didn't seem to do anything else.

"It's going really well." He'd said to me one day. "Why don't you spend more time on it, it's meant to be yours."

I laughed inwardly.

196

"I can't spend time on MY poetry website because I'm far too busy looking after OUR family and trying to find us a secure place to live," I'd thought to myself. Did he have no idea whatsoever about what was happening in the real world anymore?

"After you've been jogging today, I'm heading out myself. I'm taking up power walking," he'd announced.

Power walking? We'd been married five and a half years, and he'd never taken any exercise in that time. Now he was power walking. I shrugged it off. Then, on one of the rare occasions we were both in the same room these days; he made a 'passing' remark.

"She's the next Poet Laureate you know, so bloody talented!" He'd announced to me one day whilst I was cooking lunch for the kids.

"Who is?"

"Kitty, from the poetry site. She's recently joined. Her poems are amazing!"

I knew who he was referring to. I read some of her work, and we'd exchanged a bit of banter in the chat room on occasion. Poet Laureate though?

"Yeah, she seems quite nice," was my reply. But in the back of my mind, a seed had been planted.

I was enjoying the website, and spending what time I could on it, but the lion's share of the work was being done by Bill. This wasn't my choice. It was not how I'd wanted things to be. My plan had been to learn the ropes with Bill, working together as a team. As it worked out, this wasn't possible, because I was too tied up looking after the kids. Tim was still only six months old, and with the girls being just three and four, my time was pretty much spent on them. I was disappointed, but accepted that there was probably little hope of me getting completely involved with 'the business' for the foreseeable future. Poetry was currently the last thing on my mind anyway. I was completely preoccupied trying to figure out how we could secure a roof over our heads, and quickly.

Renting in Switzerland isn't cheap. I started looking around for something comparable to the place we were currently in, and it seemed that we would end up paying more to rent a place than the mortgage payments would be if we should buy. I decided to start scouting around for houses that were more affordable, in less desirable locations. Within a week I'd come across a place that had recently been put on the market. It was large, had a good garden for the kids, and best of all, the monthly repayments would equate to less than we were currently paying on the rental property. I asked Bill what he thought, and he agreed we should go along and take a look at the place.

We liked it. It ticked all the boxes. And it would be available by the end of October, as the current owners were building their own place in the next town which would be ready to move into by December. By now I'd reasoned to myself that I was probably going to have to take on a job in order to pay rent, whilst Bill carried on working on his various projects, or doing whatever it was Bill did. My rational in looking to procure as opposed to renting, was to get some security for the children and me. Anything we bought would have to be in my name, and I fully intended to make sure that the children would be secure should anything happen to Bill or me. The only problem was raising the money for the deposit. We simply had no capital whatsoever by now.

"We've got the fifty thousand to come back from the house," Bill had reminded me.

"I don't think we should count on that. We should treat it as a bonus."

"Well, I've got the car deal contract. I've set up a meeting with them for early November in the UK. If it goes according to plan, and there's no reason why it shouldn't, we'll have enough to cover the entire deposit, with money left over to tide us through a couple of months until 'Open the Doors' is launched. And don't forget the tree business too, Sarah. I've already had several meetings with these people and they have agreed to pay me a consultancy fee of at least ten thousand to broker a deal for them with one of my old contacts in France. I'm not worried. The only problem we have is that of cash flow."

I'd read the car dealer contract, and was satisfied it was legally sound, despite it seeming a lot to pay somebody to broker a finance deal. I knew the lawyer involved, and I knew the businessman involved. It really did seem like a plausible option. Certainly it seemed more credible than a BDSM website, or the outstanding 'Open the Doors' scenario, which was becoming less outstanding by the second.

We went back to the house for a second viewing, and this time we had a longer meeting with the agent and the current owners.

"Clearly you like the house," the agent had said. "So what is it that's holding you back?"

Bill went into charm mode instantly, and explained the 'cash flow' predicament regarding the money back from the original house (which he explained we had decided to pull out of because of the building contractors adding on thousands in hidden costs after the contract was signed). He produced his current 'contract' and pointed out that the deal would be 'sealed' by the end of November, but that we needed a place to live slightly before then. The agent had clearly been discussing this with the home owners before we arrived, and to my complete amazement she then offered us a deal.

"If you really want the house, then Mr and Mrs Schroder have agreed to loan you the deposit, for a period of twelve months, at an extremely favourable interest rate." Bill nodded his head and looked contemplative.

"Would this mean we could exchange immediately and move by the end of November?"

"Yes, it would, Mr Tate. As far as the bank is concerned, they're happy, they get their money. The loan would be a private one between yourself, your wife, and the Schroder's. We can have the Notaire draw up all the relevant documents, and complete them when we sign the house over to your wife. Would that be an option for you?" Bill nodded again.

"I think this would be a perfect solution," he replied. And I nodded too. It meant we got the house, could move in right away, and had an extra time buffer should Bill's car deal contract take longer to materialise. I thought it was a solution. I believed it would help us to finally get a roof of our own over our heads, and I agreed to go ahead with the purchase, despite everything.

Silly, silly Sarah.

Bill, by now, was completely absent from the children's lives and mine.

We shared a house, but that was as far as it went. He would reluctantly read the odd bedtime story, or do the odd bath, but it was becoming pretty clear where he preferred to spend his time, and why.

I wrote a poem about depression and posted in on my website. Kitty reviewed it. She too suffered from depression, apparently. She had struggled with emotions, medications, and the deep dark abyss that you feel when you are engaged in a battle with an unseen enemy from within. She was sympathetic to my feelings as expressed in the poem, and offered me kind and encouraging words. Bill didn't. He didn't even acknowledge I'd written it. He was too busy reviewing Kitty's poems. He spent night and day online talking to her. He made no secret of the fact.

By October, I was aware that they were talking on Skype too, as he and Claudia did. I walked into his office one day with Tim in my arms, and she saw us; we were in camera shot. She smiled and waved to my baby son and me. Something tightened in my stomach. Bill was actually getting slimmer too. He was still taking dedicated power walks each day, and he'd cut down on the amount of junk he was eating. I tried my best to ignore my suspicions; I didn't want to believe he could ever cheat on me, albeit in cyber land. I'd just had a baby after all, and despite everything I still believed he loved and respected me. I reached out to him a couple of times, but he was cold now; completely non-responsive. We were like robots. Functioning, yet not really living. I desperately tried to engage Bill in conversation. I offered to cook, bought wine, turned the TV off and asked him to join me after the kids were in bed. None of it worked. The pressure was building. The feeling of tension between us by now was tangible, so I went to the website, and talked to the members there. Not about Bill and I, just about life in general. I wrote more poems, got more involved in the site, and took some time to learn about Kitty and what made her tick. She seemed an OK kid. But a kid she was, at least to me. She was at home with her parents; her only friends were in cyber land.

She enjoyed music and poetry, and she wasn't yet sure which path her life would take. Pretty much run of the mill for many twenty-three year olds.

She seemed vulnerable, and innocent, and in awe of my husband. She hung on his every poetic word, and she made no secret of it either. Bill spent some time taking photos of himself holding a guitar or with a guitar loosely thrown over his shoulder. He took the pictures when I was out with the kids, and he posted them to his profile on my poetry website. He didn't spend much time doing anything else. The meeting for the car deal had still not taken place, there was no contracting work for the tree company, and Claudia seemed to have paled into insignificance since Kitty arrived on the scene, which meant 'Open the Doors' was now well and truly on the back burner.

The house contract was signed, the removal vans were booked, and the date was set for the end of November. I knew there was no way out, and with each passing day the realisation grew and grew in me. I sat alone each night and cried. I wondered how the hell it had come to this? How could it have all gone so horribly wrong? I thought he'd loved me, I thought he wanted to make things work between us, yet it seemed he had lost all interest now. He had found another source of supply. I know that now, but back then, I felt rejected, and utterly impotent. I felt I had to coax him through these next few months, just to get him to be able to complete one of these damn deals, and get the house secured.

I was still clinging on to the naïve and hopeless dream that if maybe he could just pull off one of his deals, he may once again change, and we may still be able to salvage something, even if it were only to be an amicable separation for the sake of the kids.

I don't think I have ever felt so trapped and helpless as I did during this time. I have no doubt that I was seriously depressed and not thinking clearly, but then it's difficult to think clearly when your world is crumbling around you, and you have the responsibility of three tiny people on your shoulders. Because with the realisation that Bill was letting me go, came the realisation that despite all his protestations to the contrary, if we were to walk away from this marriage, the responsibility of those children would fall on my shoulders alone. I felt sick with terror at the thought. I felt weak and useless, and certainly not worthy of my children. How could I have brought kids into this? Had I failed them? Was this all my fault? There were a million questions, and accusations, and recriminations, and they were all thrown at Sarah, by Sarah.

* * *

At the beginning of November, about two weeks before we were due to move to the new house, Bill told me he'd arranged the meeting to broker the car deal. It was to take place in London.

"How will we afford it?" I'd asked, panic stricken. "How the hell are we going to get through the next month at all?"

In desperation, I'd had to turn to my parents. They had agreed to lend us the money to pay for the removals company, and some other residual expenses associated with the move. I was so grateful to them, because I had no idea how to get out of any of this, so it seemed my only option was to move forward with it, get into the house, then have a serious review of the situation with Bill.

"I'll have to go," he said. "This is the brokerage deal; it's a dead cert. We need me to go, we have no choice."

I agreed he needed to go, but asked him to fly low cost, and book a B&B in London.

"You're the broker, you don't need to entertain the clients," I'd reminded him.

My mum, concerned for my mental well-being, and moreover for the well-being of her grandchildren, had transferred one thousand pounds sterling into my UK credit card account (of which Bill had a second card). This was money that was expressly sent to feed our children, as I had broken down in tears the week previously and admitted I no longer had money for groceries. Two days before he was due to fly, Bill was out on his usual power walk. I went to take something down to the office, and noticed his flight details were on his desktop. I did a double take. The meeting was scheduled for Monday afternoon, yet he'd booked a return flight for Thursday evening. What was he staying so long for? Three nights for one meeting? We couldn't afford three nights! I picked up the piece of paper to look again, and behind it was the hotel confirmation. I had to sit down. The reservation was for the Five Star Kempinski Kensington Hotel. A suite, with a Jacuzzi, number of adults: two. Price: three hundred pounds per night. It had been booked using my credit card which had been paid for with the money sent by my mother, to feed our children.

Chapter Nineteen

Trapped in a Spider's Web

I felt sick. How could he? How the hell could he do this? I was incredulous. But my incredulity had less to do with the fact he'd booked a room for *two*, and much more to do with the fact he'd booked a suite in a five star hotel, when we had no money to feed our three children! Of all the selfish, self-centred things to do! He'd used the money my mother had sent, and spent it on some five star luxuries for him and…..Kitty? Where the hell did this man get off? He hadn't earned a penny in almost a year, yet he found it OK to book a five star hotel, for four nights?? I had to catch my breath. The kids were around my feet trying to get my attention, but my mind was elsewhere. I was sweating and shaking. I could barely breathe; I was so angry and upset. I paced the floor, waiting for him to return, wondering what excuse he'd manage to come up with when I put him on the spot. Surely even he couldn't worm his way out of this one? Even he couldn't justify stealing food from his own children's mouths to finance a jolly with another woman? And what the hell was she thinking? How could she? She knew he was married, she knew we had very small children! What lies had she been spun, I wondered. He's a damn good liar, after all. A damn good liar. How stupid was I? Stupid, stupid Sarah! The proof of the pudding was right here in black and white. What a damn good liar! But I couldn't allow myself to get preoccupied with Kitty and whatever it was he thought they had going on. I was so completely blown away by the selfishness of his actions, I couldn't think about anything else, other than how a man could steal from his own children. Something inside me clicked. Something was lost in that moment. A light went on inside my head ...finally. This was about the children. You can hurt me, mate, but don't you even think about hurting my children, and stealing from them. I felt I might happily have ripped his head off, had he walked through the door in that moment. Luckily for him, I was at least able to see straight by the time he did walk in.

"I have a question," I managed to ask with relative calm.

"Yes?" He asked.

"I was just wondering. You said the meeting was Monday afternoon, but I saw your flight details, it says you're not flying back until Thursday. Why?" He shrugged his shoulders.

"They might need a follow-up meeting. There may well be questions that need answering, points clarifying. I need to be available to them."

"For four whole days?"

"Yes, for four whole days."

"Fine, and the hotel? "He looked at me, defiant.

"What about it?"

208

"I see you've booked a luxury suite in a five star hotel. May I ask why? When we don't have any money to feed our children?"

"It was the only hotel available."

"I'm sorry. You're saying it was the only hotel available in the entire city of London?"

"Yes, Sarah, the travel agent booked it. It was the only one she had available. I need to be near to the clients. If I hadn't taken this one I'd have been on the wrong side of town, too far away."

"You have got to be kidding, right?" I was starting to lose it now.

"No, I'm not kidding, it was the only hotel I could get, so I took it."

"Oh my god, Bill. Let me get this straight. My mum sent money last week, because YOU haven't earned a penny in months. She sent money so we could FEED OUR CHILDREN! And you have booked three nights in a luxury hotel, at a cost of THREE HUNDRED pounds per night, just so you can 'make yourself available' to the clients? Are you serious? How can you possibly justify this? You have stolen money from our children to finance your jolly! And how the hell are you going to pay for food whilst you're there? Come to think of it, how the hell am I supposed to FEED OUR CHILDREN whilst you are in the five star lap of luxury in London?"

He looked at me, ashen, but still defiant.

"It was all I could get. I need a break too, you know."

"You need a break? You need a *break*? Oh, well that makes it OK then! All this hard work you've been doing for the last twelve months. All this stuff you've *achieved* must have completely worn you out. Of course you need a break, Bill. You poor, overworked thing. Go right ahead. Stay for a week!"

With this I started to walk away, but he followed me.

"You don't have the monopoly on tiredness, Sarah."

"Of course not, Bill! I'm only tired because I'm being mother to our children. Clearly you are much more tired than me. You work SO much harder. You do SO much more than me, right?"

He just looked at me.

"And so of course it's OK for you to go away, and book a *double* room for yourself and your little girlfriend!"

"She's not my girlfriend."

"Oh, you know who I'm talking about then?"

"You've misunderstood. Kitty is not my girlfriend. You're just jealous of her."

"I'm jealous of her? Really? Why would that be then, Bill? Maybe because you spend time when you are supposed to be working speaking to her? Maybe because you see fit to stay up until all hours chatting to her online, instead of actually *providing* for your *babies*??!!!"

"Now you're just getting hysterical. I won't listen to this."

"No, Bill, why would you listen to silly, hysterical Sarah? Why would you listen to me when you've got a little girl at the other side of your computer screen who hangs on your every word? I mean, after all ... she *believes* your drivel!"

"You need to calm down, Sarah. It always says the number of people is two when you book a suit. It doesn't mean I booked it for two people. Get your facts straight."

And with that, he retreated to his office and closed the door. I wasn't sure how to feel. I stood there, staring at the wall. I was wondering if I'd actually imagined half of the last conversation. Had he really said there were no other hotels in the entire city of London? Had he really, in all seriousness, stood there and told me he 'needed a break'? Did I actually hear him say that all double rooms have 'two people' written on the booking form? Did he think I was stupid?

Well, I knew the answer to that one. Of course he thought I was stupid! I'd been stupid all these years, hadn't I? I'd swallowed every line he'd spun. He must have been laughing at my stupidity. No wonder he had no respect left for me. I didn't know where to turn, or what to do. Part of me still couldn't actually believe it. It made me sick with rage every time I thought about it. I tried to calm down, the kids could clearly see I was upset about something, but I couldn't stop thinking about it. I kept going over what he'd said about needing a break. He'd said I didn't have the monopoly on tiredness. What did he mean? What could I have possibly done that was so bad he felt justified in taking money from the kids to pay for a five star hotel? What on earth was he hoping to achieve? Had I spent vast amounts of our money on socialising? Why did he feel he had a right to be tired? I didn't get it. He never did anything! He'd been procrastinating for five years; all the time promising me we were on the brink of something major. Yet here we were, on the brink of total disaster, and he thinks it's OK to swan off like this? We had no money in the world! What had he been planning on doing? Taking her to a swanky hotel, then not feed her for days on end? If you're going to pretend you've got loads of money, it goes further than a hotel bedroom! The credit card was almost up to its limit! There was no way he could wine and dine anybody on that!

It suddenly occurred that he must be mentally unstable. This was the first time I'd ever thought it, but surely to goodness these actions were not those of a man of sane mind? No, there had to be something wrong with him. This wasn't all about me, surely this could not all be my fault? How did he see things? I tried to get inside his mind.

He was running away from his perceived misery. That was what this was all about. In his mind, he'd fallen in love with a woman he thought was his soul mate, only to realise she never had any feelings for him at all. She had never felt the love he'd felt, and she'd effectively rejected him. She'd thwarted him, leaving him feeling helpless and frustrated. If she had supported him, stood by him like a proper wife would have, then none of this would have happened.

"Sarah doesn't have the monopoly on tiredness. Sarah has no idea of the struggles I've had to endure in this cold and loveless marriage. If only Sarah had stood by me, I could have achieved all those things. Sarah rejected me, and now I am paying the price. I need to get away; I need to do something for me. I need Kitty; she cares. I need somebody who cares. I need somebody who really loves me for who I am."

That was what he was thinking.

And so, two days later, he left for London, proclaiming to have found a cheaper hotel at the last minute. He left me lying on the sofa, having been up for the entire previous night vomiting. He left me with the three kids to look after, and fifty francs to feed us all for the week. He left me to pick up the pieces of my life.

He called me from the airport to say he'd felt so guilty he'd spent the last one hundred pounds on the credit card to buy me Chanel products in order to 'make it up to me', but that they'd 'been confiscated at security.' He left me wondering how I could ever have believed these lies for so many years.

213

* * *

Three nights later, my friend had her arms around me, but she was gripping my shoulder hard, trying to make me take action.

"Sarah, get his bags now. Pack them. We'll put them on the doorstep. I'll stay with you tomorrow and we'll get the locks changed. I'll pay for crying out loud! Please, you have to do this now!"

"I can't!" I wailed. I knew she was right, but I was terrified, and I was so exhausted I didn't have the strength.

"You can, Sarah, and you must! This guy is poison! He's going to destroy you and the kids the way he's destroyed every other person in his life! We have to do something about this ... now!"

"I know you're right, but can't you see? If I lock him out now, things will spiral out of control! I want to try to separate from him amicably if I can! I don't feel strong enough to do this! I'm scared I might crumble, and what will happen to the kids if I fall apart? If we set the ball rolling in his absence, he won't forgive me! I don't want him to turn on us! I can't cope with any more pain!"

"Sarah, I know you're scared, but there really is no alternative! You can't seriously think of staying with him after this? He's screwing around, Sarah! He's been spinning you blatant lies for years! Enough now! It has to stop! Think of the kids!"

214

"I *am* thinking of the kids! If I uproot them now and throw him out, what will happen to them? What if it gets nasty? I can't risk damaging them! I need time to think! We're moving house next week! It's too late to cancel everything. We'd just end up with more debt if we pull out now, and nowhere to live. At least we've got a house to move to. I need to get the kids into the house and *then* tell him it's over. Don't you see that? I *must* keep things running as smoothly as possible, for the sake of the kids!"

I could see she didn't really agree. She wanted to get the kids and me away from him as quickly as possible. She'd witnessed too many tears on my part. She wanted to help me to get out of that destructive situation before I went the way Sofia had gone. It was written all over her face. But, reluctantly, she agreed with me. We decided to hold fire on splitting the family up, until we were safely into the new house, and the kids had enjoyed a peaceful Christmas.

I knew it was over. I'd known it from the moment he'd walked out of the door on the Monday. It was all different now. I may not have been strong at this point in my life. In fact, I was probably at one of my weakest points ever, both physically and emotionally. But I was no longer under any illusions. Nothing he could say to me now, no matter how fanciful or romantic, was going to change my mind about him. Every scrap of feeling had gone. There was no love, no trust, and not one ounce of respect left for this man. There was only contempt, along with bitter recrimination.

215

He called me from London.

"The meeting didn't go as well as I'd hoped," he said.

(Well, what do you know!)

"Really? What went wrong this time?"

"Herr Braun's business plan sucks, basically."

(Really? You do surprise me. Weren't you supposed to be doing that for him? Isn't that what you're getting this hefty fee for?)

"Oh dear, so what happens now?"

"All is not lost. I still might be able to recover it. Maybe in the New Year. I've promised them I'll get better figures off him and present them in January. They're interested in the concept, but we need to revisit the figures."

(This is their polite way of telling you it's over, Bill)

"So, we won't be getting the loan money any time soon then?"

"Well, no. Like I said, it will be January."

(Of course it will, Bill)

"Right."

"Will you be up when I get home?"

"I don't know. I might be. Bye." And I put the phone down.

* * *

I couldn't think straight. It was all completely out of my control, and I felt more overwhelmed than I had in my entire life. What a mess. What a complete and utter mess. He was never going to deliver the goods. He was never going to pull off any of these major deals. We would never get the deposit money by this time next year, or this time next century. I knew that once I ended the marriage, he would see himself as a victim again. Poor Bill. He'd had so much bad luck befall him, and now wife number three was about to walk away too.

How was I going to do this? What would be the best course of action? I tried to figure out ways of holding on to the house for the kids and me. It was only the deposit we needed. If he could somehow raise that (whilst I worked to pay the mortgage) maybe I could secure it. But would he see this, once he knew I was going to end it all. Would he want it to be amicable? Would he walk away from the kids and me? This was my biggest fear; the fear of being left to bring up the kids all alone, with no emotional or financial help. Surely he would not, could not, turn his back on his own children? It was clear that he no longer loved me, in fact, I wondered if he ever had. I wondered if Bill actually knew what love was. He clearly believed he did. He'd tried for so long to convince me that his feelings were so much deeper and more genuine than my own. After all, I was the one who had always been so reluctant to 'scratch the surface' of our relationship, in order to explore the depths of the real feelings he wanted us to share. But what about the children? What did he feel for them? I couldn't work it out. Obviously he had doted on Lucy, at least outwardly. But in recent times he'd spent less and less time with her, favouring instead his internet lady friends. Alice had started to capture his attention since she'd been talking. He'd taken more of an interest in her since he'd realised she was highly intelligent. He saw her as a mini-Bill now, and had often commented on her intellectual capacity, referring to Lucy as the 'scatty one, like her mum'.

He hadn't been near Tim though. It was almost as though he didn't exist. How different he was from the very hands on father he'd been when Lucy was newly born. Tim would be the least affected by what was about to happen. I reassured myself with that thought, small comfort as it was. But the girls, what about them? How would they handle the breakup of the family? And moreover, how would they fair if he really did turn his back on them as my friends insisted he would. I didn't want to believe them. I couldn't believe them. Had he turned his back on his first three children though? What had really happened? I'd never really found out what had gone on during that time of his life. Would he leave me alone with them? And if he did, would I be able to survive it? Was I strong enough to get through this?

These were the thoughts that prevented me from sleeping. And this was the reason I was still awake when he walked back through the door. I stood on the bottom stair as he came into the house. He gave me a sheepish half-smile and walked towards me. When he reached the stairs he put his arms around me, and tried to take me into them.

"I've been such a fool," he said, trying to kiss me. I pulled away.

"Yes," I replied. "You certainly have."

I turned my back on him and walked to my room, closing the door on him, and on us.

Chapter Twenty

A Christmas from Hell

Extract from my journal: 15.11.07

*'Haven't been able to bring myself to write in this journal for
months, things have been too horrible. I've probably reached
the lowest point of my entire life. Everything has fallen apart.
All my hopes and dreams of a 'Happy Ever After' have gone
out of the window. Bill hasn't earned any money at all in
almost a year. We lost the original house, and only through a
stroke of luck were able to find another one in time. He is
still working on various 'projects' but as yet none have come
to fruition. This month we reached the stage where we had
nothing left. A family of five, with no money on earth. What a
very scary place to be! And what did my husband do? He
took money mum had sent to feed the kids, and spent it on a
luxury hotel in London, so he could have some 'me' time.
(Except it wasn't just for him.) I've spent so much time
feeling furious and let down. I spent some time trying to fight,
to get onto Bill's side and make the marriage work. I tried to
help in any way I could to get this marriage on track and
save our family from this crap situation he's created for us.
Unfortunately though, the marriage is going down the toilet
in a big way. Too much has happened now. Feelings have
changed. We can never go back. I'm sinking further and
further into depression, but I'm trying my best to keep it
together for the sake of the kids, but it's getting harder each*

day, and I just don't know how much more I can take. Bill and I don't talk any more. I tried and tried over the last few months to get things out into the open, but he's lost interest. His thoughts are elsewhere now. I have no idea what's going to happen next. We move house next week. I'm terrified.'

* * *

Bill and I had completely stopped talking. We were civil in front of the children, but that was about it. He seemed genuinely upset and annoyed that I had 'rejected' him when he returned home from his week away. I could barely even bring myself to look at him. There seemed no point in trying to talk to him about our situation now. I asked him only about the necessities. About when we might be likely to see any money, how we would pay for the first months mortgage. He didn't have any answers for me, just the usual rhetoric about 'this' or 'that' project, which was in the pipeline. He assured me he'd started looking around for some contract work to tide us over. He spoke of Head Hunters and job offers a plenty. Nothing materialised though.

The home situation wasn't unbearable though; it wasn't as though we were at each other's throats. I somehow managed to put the hotel incident out of my mind, or at least to the back of it. Even in my depressed state, I knew there would be no point speaking to him about it again. I knew better than to rock the boat further. I needed to bide my time now, and try to keep things on an even keel until at least we were in the new house.

Two days before the move, I was in the house with Tim, surrounded by boxes and chaos. The doorbell rang. When I answered it, there was a man standing there in the rain, clipboard in hand.

"Mrs Tate?"

"Yes."

"Is Mr Bill Tate here?"

"No, he's out. Can I help?"

"Sign here, please." It was a familiar piece of paper by now. Another Court Order demand for money. But this wasn't the postman delivering it. This was a representative from the Government. This was the taxman. I took a deep breath, put out my hand, and signed the form. He handed me the paperwork, then shook his head. I closed the door behind me, only then daring to look at the document in my hands. It was an income tax demand for about ten thousand Swiss Francs, for the year 2004. Three years ago. So, he hadn't paid tax in 2004, and they had taken this long to catch up with him? What about subsequent years?

"I don't know what this is for." He shook his head when he read the document.

"It's for income tax, Bill. You didn't pay it."

"I can see that, Sarah, but what I'm saying is that I don't know why. Stupid bloody accountant must have made a mistake. He could get done for this!"

"So you're telling me that the qualified accountant you employ to do the books has omitted to tell you that you've failed to pay rudimentary income tax? You really think he missed this?"

"Yes, he must have done. This is the first I've heard about it."

"Well you should send the court order to him then, he should pay it." I walked away. I had to. I wondered how long it would be before the court orders arrived for 2005 and 2006. I knew there would be more. Everything was crashing down now.

I don't know how I got through the move. It was just a blur. I was existing on about two hours' sleep a night, and couldn't bring myself to eat. I knew this wasn't good, that I should try to stay healthy and functioning for the sake of the kids, but it was almost impossible. I became a robot.

Bill continued doing what Bill did. He chatted to his 'friends' on my poetry site, he surfed the web, looking for a work contract; he ignored me wherever he could and was barely interacting with the children.

As soon as we were in the new house I started to get my CV up to date and scour the job sites for work. I had no idea what I could do; I'd been out of the work place for almost five years now. The thought of handing the kids over to somebody else broke my heart, but I knew I just had to do something to pay my way. Christmas was rapidly approaching, and I'd organised nothing for the children. My parents had arranged to come to stay for the holiday, and I focused very much on getting them over. I wanted to give my kids a good Christmas. I knew it would be the last as a family. But I was wading through treacle again. I felt as though my life was closing in around me, and I was suffocating. My mum knew how desperate things had become. I'd told her about what had happened in November. She set about organising Christmas, and she and my father generously offered to pay for everything. I was so grateful to them. I knew if it hadn't have been for them, there would have been no Christmas in our house that year. There was no money for food by now. I sold Tim's pram online, and managed to get a decent price for it. I then suggested to Bill that he pawn our jewellery. I'd had a drop pearl necklace and earrings made bespoke for the wedding. They were my pride and joy, and I'd been saving them for the girls. But I knew I had no choice. The girls needed feeding more than they needed pearls. I also had some other items, mostly white gold with small diamonds. Probably about five thousand retail value, but I knew we'd get a lot less selling them on. I handed the items to Bill a week before Christmas, and asked him to see if he could sell them. He took them, returning a couple of hours later.

"Did you sell them?"

"Yes, but I only got nine hundred francs I'm afraid."

I looked at him. Then we both looked at his wrist. He was still wearing his four grand watch.

"He offered me money for it, but not enough," he said, instantly aware of what was going through my mind.

"How much did he offer you?"

"Seven hundred. I told him I'd think about it."

He told them he'd think about it? He sold my bespoke jewellery that I'd been keeping for my girls, yet he couldn't part with his watch! I didn't need to say anything to him. My look must have said it all. He turned his back and walked away. I managed to run upstairs away from earshot of the kids before I began my hysterical sobbing. Surely this couldn't be happening? What more must I see of this man, and who he really is? Did I ever know him at all? I was heartbroken. I felt worthless and utterly unloved. He'd never loved me. He couldn't possibly have done. I knew it now. What he'd just done had proved it. Why the hell had I not seen this before? How could I have been so blind?

I started to question myself again, and with the questions came more self-reproach. How could I have allowed this to happen? What the hell was I thinking of? Why was I too weak to take my friend's advice last month before we'd moved into this house? Why was I so feeble and useless? I hated myself. I'd ignored all the warning signs. I'd closed my eyes and ears. I'd ignored the advice of friends, and I'd switched off that all-important inner voice, which had been screaming at me for years. I was so bloody stupid!

For a brief moment, I wondered if life was worth living any more. Then I remembered the kids. Of course it was worth living, they needed me!

Thankfully, the children were oblivious. They had no idea of the trauma that was going on around them. They still had their mummy and daddy together in one house. They saw us speaking to each other. We were always pleasant to one another when the kids were around. We even laughed and joked. We were both pretty good actors. So to the kids, life was normal, for now. So we bought a tree and let the girls help to decorate it, and when my parents arrived they brought gifts for the Santa sacks, and paid for the entire Christmas hamper of food, wine, and other goodies.

"We'll give the kids a great Christmas," my mum had said as I'd wept on her shoulder.

"We'll put it all out of our minds. Be nice to one another for the sake of the kids. You can do that, can't you? We're here to support you. You're strong, and you're going to be fine."

Bill had helped to unpack the shopping, but had soon retreated to his new basement office, without one word of thanks to my parents.

* * *

On Christmas Eve he'd appeared in the kitchen, with his coat on.

"I'm going out shopping," he'd said. "Are we buying each other presents this year?" I looked at him, incredulous. "What with?"

"Just asking." And off he went. Still wearing his watch.

* * *

Christmas Day was another blur. The kids were excited and happy to receive their gifts, and the adults put on a show of unity as best we all could, given the circumstances. I was watching the clock, wondering when would be the earliest acceptable time to reach for a wine glass. I didn't know any other way of getting through the day. The inner turmoil was relentless. The sinking feeling in my stomach refused to go away. The sheer awkwardness of it all was horrific.

Bill was in charge of the food, as always. He took over the kitchen; it was the first time we'd really seen him upstairs since my parents had arrived. He was downing neat vodka and showing signs of amiability as the day wore on.

By lunchtime, after a few glasses of wine, even I was starting to loosen up, and there were a couple of 'normal' moments when we all spoke and made light jokes. The kids were playing around the tree; the turkey was roasting. You might have thought for a minute that all was well.

Once lunch was over though, it was a return to the norm. Bill retreated to his room, and to his internet connection.

"You'd think he'd stay and play with the kids for a while," my dad remarked.

"No, dad. There's somebody far more important on the other end of the internet chat line, or on the webcam."

I knew who he was chatting to. I heard his voice. The voice of the old Bill, the Bill I'd fallen in love with. I hadn't heard that tone in his voice for a long time, but I hadn't forgotten how charming and seductive it could sound, when you don't know any different.

Time dragged for the next few days. Four adults, all trying their best to be polite, yet the undercurrents were unmistakable. Bill stayed in his office the entire time, surfacing only to use the bathroom or read the kids the odd bedtime story. I tried to relax and enjoy the kids, yet I was becoming more and more unsettled at the thought of Bill being down there talking to somebody on the internet, rather than making an effort with his family. This was Christmas after all, and he still hadn't thanked my parents for providing for us!

I decided that being sulky wasn't going to help the situation. As usual, I knew I would have to coax him and 'keep him sweet' if I was going to get him to behave with a semblance of normality so we could get through this holiday. Once the holiday was over, I didn't care what happened. I just wanted to get through the next few days, for the sake of the children.

The weekend came, and my parents and I decided we needed to get more supplies in ready for the New Year. We made a late breakfast of bacon sandwiches before we headed out to brave the rush at the shops. I was preparing the food and brewing tea. I shouted down the stairs to Bill to see if he'd like a cup.

"Yes please," came the reply. As I made the tea and got the sandwiches ready, Bill emerged from the stairwell but headed straight upstairs to the first floor bathroom, without stopping. The shower started to run.

"He seemed in a bit of a hurry to get up those stairs," my mum remarked. I put the kids' food out and got them to the table, then decided to take Bill's cup of tea and bacon sandwich down to his office.

In his new office, Bill had placed his desk with its back to the wall, so that when you walked in the door, you could only see the back of the computer monitor. I walked around the desk though, to put the tea on a coaster he had there. I looked up at the screen. Everything was blank, except a little Skype signal that was flashing orange at the bottom of the screen. When you message somebody on Skype, their name appears in the orange box. It was winking at me. It said 'Kitty'. Normally I wouldn't have even bothered, but in that instant I just froze. I remembered him running up the stairs a couple of minutes previously, and going straight into the shower.

My mum had thought it was odd. Before I could stop myself, I clicked on the orange message box. And there it was. In full, technicolor glory.

Bill: My hands are all over you.

Kitty: OOohhhhhhhhhh

Bill: My lips are exploring you, touching you, tasting you.

Kitty: ooh yessssss!!!!!!!!!!!!!!

Bill: You're soft to touch, I breathe in your perfume. My mouth moves lower. You're warm and ready.

Kitty: Oh Bill, yes!

Bill: I want you now, right now.

Kitty:
!!

Then there was nothing. Obviously he'd gone upstairs at this point, and she was waiting.

Kitty: Bill?

Kitty: Bill, are you there?

Kitty: Bill?

I stared at it. I was shaking in anger. I felt the blood draining from my body. I could actually feel it gathering in my feet, making them heavy, unable to move. I couldn't bring myself to scroll up the page to what had been written before. I just stood there, staring. I thought I might throw up. Then, suddenly, I was moving. My legs were carrying me up the stairs. I stopped when I got to the top. My mum looked up from her lunch, and as soon as her eyes met mine she went white.

"What's happened?" I couldn't speak.

"Sarah, what's happened?" I still couldn't speak. Instead, I turned and headed up the stairs. Up to the bathroom, where he was still in the shower. I knocked on the door. No answer. I knocked again, louder this time. The water stopped running.

"Bill, open the door!" The voice was mine, but it sounded different, higher pitched. Still no answer. Now I was hammering on the door with my fist.

"OPEN THE DOOR!"

"Jesus Christ WHAT????" The door opened slightly and he put his head in the gap.

"Your little girlfriend is downstairs on Skype. She's waiting for you to put your hands all over her body. Get a bag Bill, pack it.......and GET THEHELL OUT OF THIS HOUSE!!!!!" He closed the door on me. I flew down the stairs. My mum was tending to the kids.

"Sarah, what the heck is going on? Stay calm, please! For the little ones!" I looked at the kids.

"Are you OK, mummy?" asked Lucy.

"I'm fine, sweetheart. We'll go out in just a minute, OK?"

I headed back down the stairs and into the office: back to Kitty on Skype. She was still there.

Kitty: Bill? Are you OK?

Bill: Bill's not here. His WIFE is.

Silence.

Bill: Enjoying your sordid little affair with a married man are you?

Silence.

Bill: Well, you know what sweetheart. You're welcome to him!

And with that I left it. I left it on the screen, so he could come back down and see what I had written to her. I ran back up the stairs to my bedroom, and sobbed.

Chapter Twenty-One

Raw Pain and Emotion

Nothing could have prepared me for how I would feel upon seeing what I'd just seen. No amount of telling myself I already knew, of kidding myself I wouldn't be bothered by it, could have prevented me from experiencing that tsunami of emotions. The pain and rage coursed through my body; wave after wave of utter distress and despair. I thought I might go out of my mind, it felt so bad. It was the disappointment, the absolute incredulity. It took my breath away. He was having cyber-sex with a girl thirty years younger, whilst his children played with their Christmas presents in the next room. I couldn't stop thinking about how he'd rushed upstairs to the bathroom. I felt physically sick at the cheap sordidness of it all.

So this is what we'd been reduced to? This was the man who I'd believed was worthy of his place on the pedestal I'd placed him on. Here he was, stripped naked. I saw him for what he really was, and he completely repulsed me.

A man who I'd loved, married, and had children with. The man I'd stuck with despite all the odds, and this is what it came down to in the end; A sad, pathetic cyber affair, with a young woman who didn't know any different. I pitied her. I despised him.

"You disgust me, Bill," I said after I followed him downstairs to his office.

"Say what you like." He had that defiant look in his eyes again.

"You're a pathetic, sad old man. Getting your kicks by seducing some unsuspecting young woman online. Poor kid never stood a chance, did she, Bill? I remember the flowery rhetoric well. You should be ashamed of yourself. Your children are in the next room!"

"I'm not ashamed of what I have with her. What do you care anyway? You're no longer interested in me. You've never been interested in me. You've never once tried to understand the *real* me. You just see what you want to see. You're shallow, Sarah."

"*I'm* shallow? I fell in love with you. I married you and had your babies. I've put up with much more than most women could stand to bear. And you stand there and call *me* shallow! You're the biggest disappointment of my life, Bill!"

"Well then we agree on something then, because you're sure as shit the biggest disappointment of mine, baby."

"Pack your bags and leave Bill, you make me sick."

"I'm not leaving sweetheart. I'm staying put. Make me go. Now get out of my office, please."

I stood there, shaking. He was already on the computer, trying to contact her. I couldn't believe my eyes! I turned and went upstairs, into the arms of my mother.

* * *

The next few days passed by in a complete blur. I was riding a rollercoaster of emotions, and I had no idea how to escape it all. His proximity was extremely difficult to cope with. I had to pretend in front of the children that all was well, whilst at the same time choking back tears of anger and frustration. I sought answers from him, yet got none. He was colder than he'd ever been with me, and for some unknown reason this drew me towards him even more. I was desperate to open the lines of communication somehow, if only to get some sort of reassurance that he would remain a part of the children's lives, and at least try to support us financially. I knew I couldn't do everything by myself, yet I was terrified that's what would happen.

This man had hurt me to the core. He'd ruined my life and destroyed my self-confidence. I felt utterly bereft, and unable to even contemplate a future alone with the kids without his help. It was the lowest point of my life to date, and he knew it.

* * *

On New Year's Day, we feigned a family atmosphere, for the sake of the children. We cooked a meal, and Bill joined us at the table. At the end of the meal, he addressed my parents for the first time in days. His voice was weary and monotone.

"I just want to say thank you for all you've done for us this Christmas, and in the months before. Thanks for providing the money, and the gifts for our children. I just want to reassure you that you'll get every single penny back. I will make sure you get paid back."

My parents nodded. They knew as well as I did they'd never see a penny again. He made no effort at all to repay them. He had too many other debts.

I deleted Kitty and all her work from my poetry site. I couldn't erase what he'd done, but at least I could remove that small part of it. Even though I'd never met the girl, I felt betrayed by what she'd done, but deep down I knew she was probably not to blame for this. Who knows what lies he'd spun for her? It was what he did best. I knew she'd been very depressed and vulnerable. She had written poetry about it, and it was one of the things I always felt I had in common with her. Now, in the cold light of day, I could see how she'd fallen prey to him. Because, to me, that's what she was, another of his victims; even though she didn't know it yet.

* * *

Once my parents had returned to the UK, I felt completely alone and helpless. Despite my asking Bill to leave, we both knew that was never going to happen. He had nowhere to go, and we simply couldn't afford to run two households.

"I want a divorce." I repeated this request yet again. He seemed genuinely surprised that I was even asking this.

"If you say so," was the reply, "but you're not having the kids."

"I think you'll find I am having them!" I'd retaliated.

"I'll fight you for them!" was the defiant response.

"And you honestly think you'll win? With your track record? Do me a favour, Bill!" I was shaking with emotion. I couldn't actually believe I was hearing this!

"Well, I'll take Lucy then, you can have the other two." I stood there, open-mouthed. Had he really just suggested we split the children between us? Did I honestly just hear those words come from his lips? I looked at him, and he was standing there awaiting my response. He'd really suggested it, and he really meant it.

In that moment, I knew the man was completely unhinged.

What the hell had I been doing with this person? Who the hell was this person standing before me? What the hell was going to happen to this family now? I simply didn't know which way to turn. I tried to focus on some practical things, but it was difficult even to concentrate on the most mundane of tasks. I was in an impossible position. Three small children, up to my neck in debt, no job, and no way out. It felt like a dead end street. And all the while, Bill was there, living in the basement, and carrying on his little 'cyber sessions' with his girlfriend, right under my nose. It was almost too much to bear. I needed release, so I started writing:

Words, song lyrics:

Words come so easy to people like you
When words flow with ease, they don't need to be true
Creating a world, a fictitious story
Becoming a God in your kingdom of glory

Your words are so empty, be they written or spoken
These words can't make love, and our love is broken

A wonderful hero, a spectacular mind
Words upon words, no substance behind
But here in the real world, words aren't enough
They give no support, when the going gets tough

Your words are so empty, be they written or spoken
Your words can't heal love, our love is so broken

Here in the land of the living and breathing
Reality's hard, there are mouths that need feeding
Actions speak louder than words in this life
Your actions destroyed us, they cut like a knife

Your words are so empty, be they written or spoken
These words can't save love, and our love is broken

Promises promises, I've heard them for years
Words and more words, they fall on deaf ears
Empty and void, your words are so shallow

No longer ring true, they are lifeless and hollow

Your words are so empty, be they written or spoken
These words can't heal love, our love is so broken

So I listen no more to the romantic dream
I can take it no longer, your words make me scream
So go forth and conquer, imaginary Knight
Find another young mind, your words to excite

Your words are so empty, be they written or spoken
These words won't save love, our love it is broken

Write some more words, but leave me in peace
Keep living your dreamland, just give me release
Further and further, you're fading away
You ran and you hid, left me in today

Your words are so empty, be they written or spoken
These words can't heal love, our love is so broken

Linguistic expression can't repair what you've done
Run along to your tart now, for my love has gone....

I posted my lyrics and poems on the website. The members
knew what had gone on. I had talked to anybody and
everybody who would listen to me. I reached out via internet
and by phone. I went over and over it with friends from far
and wide. I received counselling and coaching from people
I'd known for years, and from people I'd never even met.

When I look back now, I think this is what helped to save
me. My ability to express myself and let all the emotion out

as it was happening to me. I opened up to people and bared my battered and broken soul. I accepted offers of condolence and emotional support, and I didn't think twice about it.

I'm glad it all came pouring out of me the way it did. I had no reservations about telling people what had happened. As embarrassed and ashamed as I was (for I still blamed myself for much of what had gone wrong), I suddenly found a capacity to expose my soft underbelly to the world, and shout 'yes, I'm hurting, please help me.' And the help came pouring in; it was overwhelming. I let it wash over me, because I knew this was what I needed to give me the strength to make that final break. I knew things were going to get more difficult from now on. As much as I didn't want to consciously admit it, I was aware in the pit of my stomach that I was going to have to take complete control of the situation from now on, and if the children and I were to escape this mess he'd created for us any time soon, I would have to get myself together, and get into the driving seat.

My first step was to initiate divorce proceedings. I knew I needed to get some legal advice soon. I made an appointment for us to both visit our lawyer at his practice. I knew we couldn't afford to go into battle legally, and as there were no money or assets to divide, as long as we could keep things relatively amicable, there was no reason why we shouldn't just use the one lawyer.

In the meantime, Bill was still 'working' on whatever projects he was 'working' on. Except, it seemed, 'Open the Doors'.

"What happened to the Open the Doors scheme?" I asked one day.

"Nothing. We've decided to hold off on it for now. Claudia has another big project coming up which will take up all her time. I need to concentrate on getting money in to get us out of this mess. So we've left it for now."

It was a bog standard Bill answer, which I was used to hearing by now. It signalled to me that their relationship was also over. I wondered if there were more to it. Had they had a falling out? Or was it was a genuinely amicable parting of the ways? In my experience, not many people ever parted ways with Bill amicably. I wondered if Claudia had seen through him. Had she got tired of waiting for his words to turn into actions? Probably, but, as with many other things, I resigned myself to never knowing the full extent of what had happened between them. I had no time to worry about it, though; there were far more pressing things going on.

The 'follow up' trip to London was looming. Bill claimed to have anew and re-worked business plan from Herr Braun. Apparently this was the chance to finally get the money that would secure the house.

"I really have to go, it's our only hope of getting the house secured," he said.

"Well go then. But book a B&B, and come back the next day." I knew deep down he had no chance of getting the contract. He hadn't succeeded at a thing in the entire time I'd known him; why would now be any different? But there was always a sliver of hope in my stomach that I might still be wrong, and he might just be able to pull this one off.

But it was the start of another series of blows, and I wasn't in a strong enough place to deal with any more of it. Who was I trying to fool? Of course he came back empty-handed, and he didn't even care that he'd booked and paid for the trip on my overstrained credit card once again. When I got the invoice I almost had to laugh. Restaurants, a purchase at a high street books store, and a visit to the Tate Gallery. The fact that he'd spent the three weeks before his trip setting Kitty up with her own website was bad enough, but when I looked on her site and saw her enthusing about her recent trip to the Tate Modern, I turned the emotion in on myself. I hated myself all over again.

How could I continue to act like such a doormat? What self-respecting woman allows herself to be treated like dirt in this way? These two were laughing at me. They must have been laughing their way all around the Tate Gallery!

* * *

And he blogged on his own website. And like a stupid lamb to the slaughter I read his words. He wrote of meeting his soul mate, his one true love, just a few months ago. He wrote poetry about her, declared his undying love. He created a website with photos he'd taken and thoughts he'd written, and nowhere did he mention Lucy, or Alice, or Tim. Nowhere did he acknowledge that he had three of the most beautiful children in the world. He talked only of her, of his one soul mate.

* * *

Self-loathing is the most dangerous form of depression. You convince yourself that everything that has happened is because of you. You believe yourself to be your own worst enemy, and you feel that nobody could benefit from your existence on the planet.

I'd been stripped bare. There was nothing left. I was functioning for the sake of my children, yet I was barely there as a person in my own right. I was losing control, and I saw no way of regaining my life. I wasn't worthy of my children. They deserved better. I had brought this all on myself. I was being a victim. I lived to be a victim. I could never be a strong and beautiful person, because I was weak and pathetic. I'd allowed this to happen to me because of the type of person I was. I was looking for misery. I wanted misery. I must be craving it, and now the universe had delivered it. Misery. It was no more than I deserved. So I turned the anger in on myself, and I began a pattern of behaviour that would last for many months. I binged and purged. Binged and purged. It was my release. It was the only control I had left. But it sent me spiralling down even further, and I came as close as I've ever done to the brink.

* * *

I felt Sofia's pain, because I shared it now. I started to realise what she might have gone through in those last weeks. The feeling of complete rejection: of utter helplessness. You've been pushed down into the depths, and whilst you're down there, he comes back and kicks again. It's relentless, and you feel utterly at his mercy. It's the scariest place I've ever been. And I finally understood why she did what she did. I'd always wondered how anybody could get so desperate that they would do anything, absolutely anything, just to be set free. Now I understood. But I knew I couldn't take the option she had taken. I knew I had to fight, for the sake of those three innocent children, who had never asked for any of this. I pulled myself back, and I went and held my babies. I knew I'd never let them go. I'd save them, and they in turn, would save me. So I tried to gather my strength, what was left of it, and get myself back onto some sort of form again. I knew the only way I could survive this would be to somehow toughen up a bit. Yet I felt so weak and helpless. The fact that we were still under the same roof, even though he lived his life entirely in the basement now, was driving me crazy beyond belief. His presence sucked my energy from me, and I started to hate him for it.

"Hold on to the hatred, hold on to the anger!" my mum had shouted at me one day over the phone.

"Stay mad! It will drive you through this! Focus your negative energy on *him*! He's the one who's in the wrong, Sarah, not you! You *must* start to believe that!"

She must have felt so helpless, being so far away and only able to offer words for comfort. There was no practical help anybody could give. But the words helped, they really did.

* * *

Bill finally got a contract at the end of January. At last there would be money coming in once more, and we could start to make moves to finally separate. It was ironic really, because the contract was working in a large Swiss bank, in the credit control department.

"It's meant to be a six month contract, but they've already told me they'll need me for at least a year, and most likely beyond," he told me gleefully after just one week on the job.

"It's good money, so we may still be able to save this house for you and the kids. I was thinking I could get a small studio apartment nearby, and we'll be able to share custody. I think that could work."

"Of course it will work, Bill," I'd thought to myself. "Just like everything else you've ever suggested."

I wondered how anybody could live in such a deluded place. Did he have no common sense whatsoever? Did he actually believe his own hype? Or was he secretly just taking the Mickey out of me the entire time?

The following Monday, as I sat with Tim, looking around the sparsely furnished house, wondering how quickly and painlessly I could get myself and the kids out, the doorbell rang again: And I took delivery of three more court orders. Tax for 2005 and 2006, and a demand for non-payment of pension funds, for both Bill and myself: three years' worth.

Chapter Twenty-Two

Trying to Gather Strength

"Are you sure this is what you want, Sarah?" The solicitor looked at me. I looked over at Bill, who shrugged his shoulders.

"Yes. I'm positive."

"OK, well if you're sure. No mediation, nothing?"

"No. Divorce please."

"OK, if that's what you're both agreed on?" He looked at Bill, who slowly nodded.

"Right, then we need to draw up an agreement to provide to the Judge. We will submit the documents, then you will be summoned to appear before him. As long as you both agree on the terms of the agreement, he will grant a separation. After that, you wait three months, and the divorce then becomes final."

"Good, let's do it," I said.

"We need to know details of your financial situation, so we can draw up a plan for a separation of assets."

"There are no assets, there is only debt." I said. He didn't look surprised.

"How much debt?" He asked. I looked at Bill, who frowned.

"Excluding the house and the private loan for the deposit about eighty thousand, give or take," he told the Solicitor.

"OK Bill, well we need to know the true extent so we can see how best to divide it up."

"What am I liable for?" I asked.

"Fifty percent of all marital debts. Obviously the house is in your name, but the mortgage is joint, so again it's fifty percent. With the credit cards etc., obviously you're in for one hundred percent, as they are in your name."

I sighed. I was in for fifty percent of a debt I had nothing to do with creating. Well, maybe I did help to create it, by being so apathetic for so long. I started to cast my mind back over the events since we'd met. Looking back now, knowing what I did, made it all suddenly start to come clear. It was like somebody had lifted a veil, and I started to recognise things which had been said in the past for what they really were. Lies, lies, and more lies. It had begun the very first day we met, and it continued to this day. I wondered if he knew himself what was fact and what was fiction. I can only assume that the way he exists is to convince himself that what he says is true. In order to lead a life so fabricated and fantasy based, you must believe your own fabrication and fantasy. How else could you exist? I could see it now, how clearly I could see it. Why oh why had it taken me so long? Not any more though. Now I was taking action. The ball was rolling at last, and we had a solicitor on the case.

* * *

Early in February, whilst dining at a friend's house, I was asked if I thought Bill had really carried on a full-blown relationship with Kitty.

"Why do you ask?" I queried.

247

"Just curious. I wondered if you thought it was just a cyber-relationship, or whether they did actually meet."

"Well, he spent all that money on a hotel, didn't he? And he was blatant about his trip in January, so I'd say yes. Sad as it is. The man has no conscience."

"Damn right he doesn't," came the reply.

"Why are you asking me this?"

"Well, Sarah, I was debating whether or not to mention this, but I went out for a drink with Bill the other week, and he said some things to me which really made me change my opinion of him. In fact, I was shocked to the core."

"What?"

He hesitated.

"Oh come on, you can't 'half' tell me something. If there's something I need to know, you have to tell me it all."

"OK, well I know for a fact that he met with her, and they slept together."

Despite everything, I felt that familiar stab of pain.

"He bragged to me about the style of sex they had. He asked me if I'd ever done it that way, and kept going on and on about how sensational it felt."

More pain, and huge amounts of adrenalin started to course around my body again. My heart started pounding. Why was he telling me this?

"He showed me a picture of her, Sarah. She has long, dark hair,. She was lying on her front. Naked, and asleep. She clearly didn't know she was being photographed."

Shock now; complete, utter shock and nausea. I felt sick. Sick to hear the words he'd used to brag about their sexual encounter, and sick to know he'd taken trophy pictures to show to people. Moreover, the way he'd chosen a friend of mine to share this little gem of information. He was probably banking on it getting back to me. He knew it would cause maximum pain and distress. And it did. It hurt like hell. I was shaking like a leaf. I felt sorry for Kitty in that moment too. How hideous, to be treated like a piece of meat. To be used and then bragged about. To have your naked photograph shown to strangers: how truly awful for her, how truly sickening of him.

"Why are you telling me this?"

"Because, Sarah, I worry that despite everything, you still blame yourself. You are not to blame. This man is a slime ball. He used you and he used her too. Real men don't behave the way he has behaved. He doesn't deserve a single tear more from you. You are so far above this person. You deserve so much better. Stop feeling guilty and get angry with the bastard, because that's what he is. A bastard! Sarah, we've all suspected for some time that he was a liar. He used to brag to us about being an arms dealer. He would tell us in all seriousness that he was raking in millions. He is clearly deluded, and dangerous. For your own sake, you need to get away as quickly as possible. You've started the ball rolling now. Don't lose faith. You are doing the right thing, and we are all behind you one hundred percent."

* * *

I knew my friend was right. In my wildest dreams, I'd never imagined that Bill could stoop so low. I felt sick to my stomach, but once again full of resolve. I had to gather my strength now. I had to stop feeling sorry for myself, and get the kids and myself away from this person. Nothing he'd ever told me had been true. It was too difficult to get my head around it all now. When had it all begun? Where could it all possibly end? Had anything been real? Was it all just a complete lie? Did he ever feel anything for me? Did he ever feel anything for our children?

* * *

I thought about his first three children. How he'd told me what a bitch their mother was. How he'd made me feel sorry for him for being treated so badly by her. He'd said his decision to leave them behind and start a new life abroad was for their sakes, to spare them from being caught up in their fighting. Was any of this true? Unlikely, it seemed. What had he put her through? And moreover, what had really happened with Sofia? What had he put Sofia through, I wondered. She had taken her life in the most horrific way imaginable. You don't do something like that unless you're utterly desperate. I wondered if any of the stories about her being his accountant and it being a marriage of convenience were true. Unlikely, it seemed. But could I face knowing the truth about her? She was on my mind more and more. I couldn't stop thinking about all the things he'd said about her, about the way she'd supposedly ripped him off for all that money. How her mother was a prize bitch, who had encouraged her daughter to screw him over for hundreds of thousands of Euros. I could no longer believe this was true. In my mind, I already knew this, but I found myself more and more tempted to contact her relatives to find out for sure. I needed to know.

But not yet. First, I knew I had to get away. Now he was earning, I knew I had to seize the opportunity to get the house onto the market and get a roof over the kids' heads and mine.

A friend of mine was living away from Switzerland, and she had an empty apartment to let. I practically begged her to let me and the kids move in, just so that I could get away as quickly as possible. She was reluctant; she knew Bill's history, but in the end she let me go to her apartment as a favour, and we negotiated a knock-down rent, which Bill reluctantly assured me he would pay.

He was to remain in the marital home for the time being. It didn't really make sense, and if I'd stopped to think about it, I might have seen that, but I was just so desperate to get away, I would have done anything.

A week before I was due to move out, I got a call from the couple who we'd bought the house from:

"Sarah, I'm so pleased to have got you. We've been trying to reach Bill but he doesn't answer his telephone or emails. Is everything OK?"

"Actually Mrs Schroder, things aren't OK. We're splitting up, and we're going to have to sell the house."

"Oh no!" She was clearly shocked.

"I knew something must be going on. We've not received a single interest payment on the loan yet."

"You've not received anything? Are you sure?"

"Positive, Sarah, and if we don't get a payment soon, we'll have to call in the debt, all of it. We're building our own house, you know, and our bank needs to see that this money is coming in."

My heart sank. Bill had assured me that he'd made these payments. These people had trusted us, and I was very aware of their own situation. That he hadn't even made one payment was unforgivable. The instalments were only a couple of hundred Swiss francs per month.

"I really don't know what to say, Mrs Schroder. I'll try to organise a payment for you, and I'll keep you posted about developments with the house sale."

I called the Real Estate Agent straight away, and organised for the house to be put on the market again with immediate effect; we only had six months before the balance of the loan was due. I hoped and prayed we could sell it in this time, and cancel out the mortgage and private loan debts.

Just before I moved out of the house, the preliminary divorce papers arrived. The financial proposal was pretty simple. It divided Bill's current salary exactly in half, giving him fifty percent, and me and the kids the other fifty percent. Considering I'd had to sign to accept fifty percent of his debt, I thought this was more than reasonable. But he was reluctant to sign.

"This settlement states that I pay you alimony as well."

"Yes, that's what you agreed when we were with the solicitor. I want to go to work, Bill, and I will, but in the meantime I need something to live on. The kids aren't even in school yet, so it's going to be almost impossible to get

252

work before they start. The childcare costs will be too much. We can't afford the private kindergarten any more, you haven't even paid the fees the last two months so I'll have to take them out of there too, which means I'll have them full time until school starts I'm just asking for help until I can have a chance to get on my feet."

He shrugged. I could tell he wasn't happy about it, but he signed the papers and I immediately sent them to the solicitor. Two days later I received an invoice from the Court for its costs, to be paid up front. I knew we didn't have the money, so I called my parents.

"How much?" My dad had asked.

"Two grand."

"Where shall I send it?" So keen were my parents that I was to get this divorce, they once again sent their pension money to Switzerland to keep things moving.

* * *

The day the kids and I were to leave, Bill took a rucksack and headed off to Zürich to spend the weekend with a work colleague. He had that ashen look once again. I felt momentary sympathy and regret. But I knew I had to move forwards.

Immediately after we moved into the new apartment, I started to feel I might be getting stronger. I was finally away from that most oppressive of environments. I no longer had to face him every day, and listen to him in his cellar, still trying to impress the ladies on the other end of the internet line. I no longer had to witness his physical deterioration. He'd let himself go completely now. The man who had taken such pride in his appearance when we had first met, who had refused to wear anything but designer clothes and the best aftershaves. He was now a shadow of that man. He was unkempt, overweight, grey and old looking. He hadn't changed his bedclothes in three months.

* * *

For me, freedom hadn't come a day too soon. I don't know how much longer I could have gone on living with him. It was driving me crazy, literally. Now I had to explain things to the kids though, and that wasn't easy.

"Mummy and daddy don't love each other anymore, so we've decided it would be best if we live apart from now on. We still love you three though, with all our hearts, and nothing is going to change that, I promise."

"Why have you stopped loving each other, mummy?"

"Sometimes grownups just do, sweetheart. There are lots of reasons why this happens. It's just the way things are. We still love you though, you must believe that."

"Are you angry with daddy?" I didn't know quite how to answer that one. So I decided on honesty.

"Yes, sweetheart. I'm angry with daddy. I'm not angry with you though. You've done nothing wrong."

"Is that why you cry so much mummy?" My eyes filled with tears.

"Yes, sweetheart. That's why mummy cries. But I'm OK; you mustn't worry. Everything is going to be OK." And I held them close, and tried to find belief inside me, that things really would be OK. We were on our own now; we had taken that first step and were away from his daily influence. But we were by no means free of him, not yet. We were still one hundred percent reliant on him. He paid our rent that first month, but then gave me only four hundred Swiss francs to live on. Once again, my parents had to chip in to keep us all fed. Bill's reason for only being able to give us this much was that the County Courts were demanding money for the unpaid taxes, and because we weren't yet officially separated, they refused to acknowledge that we had two households. The sooner I got the judge's signature, the better.

I'd seen Bill's first wage receipt in March when it had come. I saw that the figure on it was fourteen thousand Swiss francs, yet when I'd asked him how much money he'd got, he told me it was thirteen thousand. Another lie. It never stopped.

So things weren't OK, not really. I was still struggling to deal with everything that had happened. And trying my best to come to terms with the revelation that I'd never known the man I married. I was still trying to face up to the fact that I was going it alone with three kids and the knowledge that they would be relying on me one hundred percent.

I guess I knew deep down in the pit of my stomach, that it would only be a matter of time now before we were completely alone, in every way. I knew it would have to be that way. I accepted that it would be better that way, but it still terrified me. At night it was worst. When the kids were in bed, I sought comfort from friends, but found none. I reached for the bottle, but it didn't drown my sorrows, instead exacerbating them. I reached for the fridge door, and then for the bathroom door. And still, none of it made any sense. None of it. The voice was there again, inside my head. She whispered to me one night, as I lay exhausted and empty on the bathroom floor.

"Get some answers, Sarah; you deserve some answers. Do it soon…"

So, the next day, feeling weak and drained. I searched my old Emails for the address of Sofia's brother, Rich. I found the old Email we'd received from him when we lived in France, and I drafted him a mail:

Dear Mr Martin

I dug up your Email address from an old mail to Bill, which was received to my account back in 2005. You don't know me, but I am the third 'ex Mrs Tate'. I met Bill in October 2000, nine months after Sofia's death. I was aware of Sofia of course, but knew very little about her, her marriage to Bill, and the events leading up to her death. To be honest, I'm not even sure what I'm hoping to achieve in contacting you, and I do apologise if I'm opening old wounds. I just feel that, knowing what I now do about Bill, and knowing the few facts I do about his past, I need some more information, for my own peace of mind. I won't bore you with my story. Just know that I am only now starting to understand Sofia and what she might have gone through. I was always led to believe that Sofia and Bill were business partners (and good friends), and that their marriage was purely for 'tax purposes'. I was told that she was his Accountant, and that she managed all of his financial affairs whilst he lived in Germany. I was also told that she had taken out a loan for a significant amount of money, without Bill's knowledge, and that after her death, this loan defaulted to him. This was the reason given tome for a German Bank demanding money from him in 2003, which he was unable to pay, and led to him putting all 'assets'(there weren't any!), bank accounts, and company ownership, into my name. At that time the only 'asset' I know of, was the house in France, which you inherited a part of when it was sold. I was also led to believe that Sofia had 'taken' money which was supposed to have been allocated to Bill's first three children, in order to finance the purchase of a house in Germany for her mother. My question, I suppose, is this. What can you tell me about Sofia's side of the story? I recall an Email from you which he showed me in 2005, in which you seemed very angry on Sofia's behalf. I supported Bill then, and accepted his explanation that you had been 'poisoned' by Sofia's mother, who (he said) was bitter towards him. I now doubt that anything I was told was true. I do not intend to use any information you may give me in any way, other than to reassure myself that I am not going crazy, and that what I have done is really the best thing for my children. I certainly have no intention of ever telling Bill I contacted you. To be honest, I'm hoping he will soon disappear from mine and my children's lives, as I believe that to be the best thing for their long term well-being. I have been left with a considerable debt. I was naive, but I am rectifying that now. Any information you give me will be used only for me unless you express otherwise, and for my children, when the time comes. Right now they are too young to understand what is happening, yet I feel that one day it is important that they know the truth about their father. Once again, I apologise if this is painful for you in anyway, and I will fully understand if you choose to ignore this mail.

Regards

Sarah Tate

I waited a day or two before I could find the strength to send it. I was like a small child pressing its finger on a fountain, knowing full well that when I released it, the water would gush out all over me. I finally plucked up the courage to send it one morning, and was amazed when the reply came back less than two hours later. I opened the mail, and got a shiver down my spine when I read its first line.

Dear Sarah

Your Email has come a little earlier than expected, but I had a feeling one day such a message might come........

Chapter Twenty-Three

Truth Hurts

I almost had stop right there, but when I tried to move I found I was glued to my chair, my eyes riveted to the monitor:

'... ...I will reply to you in detail but right now its midnight here and I have had a long day so I would ask your indulgence for me to reply more fully. I doubt you are crazy despite the fact that you probably were a bit mad to fall for Bill's tricks, but you were not the first and unless someone stops him probably will not be the last. Bill is one of those sad individuals who preys on women and leaves them with debt in every way. Moral, physical, financial and even spiritual. I tried hard to get my sister to leave him and come to stay with me in Australia but she was too deeply attached to him. Bill has stolen my sister's life. He even stole my kids European bank accounts. Anyway I must rest now but I would like to talk with you as my business with Bill is not yet finished. I pity him as he is not a man but that will not prevent me from taking care of what is owed at some stage. It is good to hear from you and I would be happy to hear more about what happened. Until I get a chance to write more I wish you all the best. You are not crazy and it sounds like you got off lightly compared to what he could have cost you. With best wishes until next week.

Richard Martin'

I read it over and over. I was shaking from head to toe. The kids were trying to get me to play with them, but I was dumbstruck. I snapped at them. I couldn't take it in.

"What the heck is wrong with me?" I shouted to myself. "This is exactly what you were expecting, isn't it? Why are you so shocked?"

But it was like the incident with Kitty. 'Knowing' it in your mind and actually 'seeing' it for yourself are two different things entirely.

Two days later, the second Email from Australia came:

'Hello Sarah

Sorry that I don't have a lot of time to write today as business demands its share of my attention. From what I know Sofia's mother gave a lot of money to help establish the business back in Germany in the late eighties and early nineties, Bill and his cohorts lived it up and operated very impressively. When I first visited them I was taken in by how they could afford the expensive cars, expensive office fit out and lifestyle. It was all coming from Sofia's mother. Bill was pretending big time but there was nothing much behind it. As a businessman I was incredulous of the way they operated but thought that perhaps they had substantial backing and that the business was for real. When I heard how they had chartered a steamboat to cruise Lake Constance to show off I knew there was something not right. My sister sadly at that time did not confide in me and kept borrowing from her mum. She could not bring herself to see that Bill was ruining her life and clung to the belief that he loved her. I cannot recall when they moved to France but I know that it was because the German banks were after them. From what Sofia told me,

Bill was seeing another woman (perhaps more than one) for some time in the late nineties and that she was trying to start a small book shop in Toulouse. However she had no capital and I think in the end was living from hand-outs from friends. Silly girl was too proud to ask me for help which would have been forthcoming. I spoke to her a couple of months before her death and tried to persuade her to come and stay with me in Australia. Regretfully she declined the offer and things went downhill from there. Bill reduced an intelligent, likable and decent young woman in dignity and self-respect to the point where her suicide was virtually inevitable, and for this I will blame him. She gave him her trust and he abused it endlessly. Bill seems to live in a world of make believe that is hard for a normal person to understand. Innately clever and cunning, he uses his not inconsiderable gift of the gab to inveigle himself and to gain trust. Sadly it sounds like he worked you over too but at least you have escaped with your mind and body intact. The property in France was indeed sold and I received a very small sum that part covered the bank accounts that Bill had stolen from me. I do not know what Sofia's mum got but she was deserving of every penny that is for sure. She is a very decent person and did not deserve to lose her only child in this way.

So how much did he drag you in for? Sounds like you had children with the man also. That must make things doubly hard for you. In reality I will not actively search Bill out, but I have the feeling that one day our paths will cross and I will not avoid him. One way or another he will come unstuck. Happy to talk more but have to do some work now. Feel free to ask any questions you like.

Best rgds

Rich'

Oh boy, did I have plenty of questions! I could think of nothing else. Here it was at last, the rock solid proof of what I'd been suspecting for some time. This man was incapable of normal human emotion. He had gone through his entire life lying and cheating. He had preyed on women and used them for his own gain. He had left a trail of destruction and broken lives, and even death, in his wake. And still it continued. How on earth did he sleep at night?

Rich had obviously been sitting in Australia thinking of little else either, because it was only a few hours later that the next mail came in:

'Hello again Sarah

I have a little more time now over my afternoon cup of coffee. I was curious about how you were told that Bill and Sofia were business partners and the marriage was for tax reasons. No doubt Bill got Sofia to sign documents. She would have done anything for him. Wish my wife had been so trusting although I would never have dreamt of leaving a woman with my debts. Too much pride to do that. Frankly I think Bill suffers from sort of delusional illness if you can call it that. I believe he actually believes his own words even though they have no basis in reality. Anyway here more of what I know:

I was always led to believe that Sofia and Bill were business partners (and good friends), and that their marriage was purely for 'tax purposes'. I was told that she was his Accountant, and that she managed all of his financial affairs whilst he lived in Germany.

262

In 1990 I was present when Sofia married Bill and in the absence of her father gave her away. Wish I had never done that. There was no talk at all of anything being done for tax reasons. We had spent some days living in their apartment and it was obvious that they had been living together as a couple for some time. To me they gave the impression of being a happy couple and Bill was quite affable. He told me what a bitch his previous wife had been and how he had now found true happiness with my sister. I found we had similar tastes in humour and he sucked me right in. He was involved in aviation industries he claimed and as a pilot myself, this was of interest. Looking at their business I was impressed and assumed it was all doing very well with major contracts in hand. Little did I realise that they were living way beyond their means on promises that by and large never materialised. Still Bill and his English business partner spent big impressing. Not sure what happened to that Partner but I was told he wanted out. I doubt that Sofia was managing his affairs other than helping by persuading her mum to lend them her hard earned money. Sofia's mum was not wealthy and had a fairly hard time as a single mother. She earned every penny she had the hard way from what I could see.

I was also told that she had taken out a loan for a significant amount of money, without Bill's knowledge, and that after her death, this loan defaulted to him. This was the reason given to me for a German Bank demanding money from him in 2003, which he was unable to pay, and led to him putting all 'assets' (there weren't any!), bank accounts, and company ownership, into my name. At that time the only 'asset' I know of, was the house in France, which you inherited a part of when it was sold.

This is just utter bullshit. If anything it was the other way around. Very convenient about putting the assets in your name. I knew that there were none other than the house. There were only debts.

I was also led to believe that Sofia had 'taken' money which was supposed to have been allocated to Bill's first three children, in order to finance the purchase of a house in Germany for her mother.

My understanding is that if any such money ever existed then Bill had long removed it for his own benefit. He even screwed his own parents by letting them invest their life savings into the house in France, on the understanding that they could live there for the rest of their days. They approached me to see what I knew about things and were bereft at how they had lost everything to Bill's mismanagement. Sadly I was unable to assist them. Sofia had set up a couple of accounts for my kids in Germany and I gave them money so that one day my children could come to Europe and have something to draw on. Bill helped himself to those funds.

My question, I suppose, is this. What can you tell me about Sofia's side of the story?

Well hopefully the above will help you to see this creature for what it really is. A pitiful thing that is a failure as a man and in its delusional state finds its way through life by preying on gullible women (sorry but I say it in the knowledge that for a while he had me sucked in too). He is very good at it but in the end no one can permanently get away with so much lying and not be found out. When that happens he moves on and creates a whole new web until it comes unstuck yet again. Sad that he has not used his not inconsiderable talents to better ends. He could have been a successful business person but without any ethics he was bound to fail.

I recall an Email from you which he showed me in 2005, in which you seemed very angry on Sofia's behalf. I supported Bill then, and accepted his explanation that you had been 'poisoned' by Bill's mother, who (he said) was bitter towards him

In fact I had very little to do with Sofia's mum at that time having only met her at the time of the wedding. My information came from Sofia's cousin after her death. It took them a long time to contact me. As soon as Bill heard of Sofia's death I understand he raced to the house in France, removed what he wanted and burned all remaining papers. He carefully formatted hard drives on PCs so that no record of her Emails, addresses etc remained. Sofia's mum had every right to be angry towards him. My understanding was that even to the last he had persuaded Sofia that he was returning to be with her for Christmas and bringing money for food etc the love struck woman believed him to the end. When it dawned on her that it was yet just another load of bullshit she could take it no more. Self-respect and dignity gone she crumbled and saw no other way than to leave this world. After that you bet I was and still am angry. I needed no one to poison my mind against him. Whilst I had suspected that not all was well and by then knew he was messing around with other women, I never thought he would reduce my sister to such penury. When I heard of her sad end I was struck numb. It was so strange as I was in France shortly after her death and totally unaware as to what happened. Perhaps it was good because I might have been motivated to go after Bill in my grief and anger then. However as I said I still have business outstanding with him if it ever works out. It would be great if he ever came to Australia and I got to know about it. I doubt he could look me in the eyes though if we meet again. Whilst I yearn to punch his lights out I am probably more interested to help others identify him for what he is and if anything could be done to stop him from repeating these endless predatory actions towards unsuspecting women. Perhaps some thought could be given to setting up a small website highlighting his "achievements". These days we all tend to Google names of those we are interested in. This made me think to Google Bill and he has a web page. I could not believe the cheek of this creature on reading his pseudo-scientific claptrap and lousy poetry.

Cheers Rich'

Reading words like this, written about the man you've married and have kids with, is tough. It doesn't matter how wronged I felt, and how much I told myself I had seen him for what he really was. The truth was, I hadn't.

There was nothing in Rich's mails that came as a surprise, yet everything in his mails rocked me to the core. That voice I'd been hearing all these years, it had been right. Was it my voice, or was it Sofia's? He had destroyed her, and in doing so he had destroyed her mother's life too, and no doubt the life of his 'friend' in France who'd discovered Sofia's body. The ripple effect was enormous too. So many people affected by his actions. So many people left bereft and devastated. And then there were his parents. How on earth was I going to come to terms with that one? I'd stood by him as he evicted them. I defended him vehemently against what I saw as their cruel betrayal of him. Yet all the while it was he who had betrayed them, in the worst way possible. No wonder the villagers had despised us. I hung my head in shame and despair. What on earth had I done? And moreover, what on earth was I going to do now?

The email exchanges with Richard, and the ensuing friendship which I developed with him, enabled me to face some of the demons that had been haunting me. Now it was all out in the open, there was nothing left to fear. There were to be no more nasty surprises. I had Bill's measure now. Knowledge is power. And I quickly began to realize that getting in touch with Richard had been the best thing I could have done. I had now been able to fill in all the gaps, and piece together the jigsaw puzzle of Bill's life. I needed no more information than I already had. The knowledge gave me strength. I knew I wasn't to blame, despite what he made me feel. This had been the pattern of his life. I had not caused him to behave in this way. He would have done this to our family anyway, because he simply could not have helped himself. This wasn't about me being a bad wife or a poor mother. Nothing I could have done would have prevented this. I knew that now.

I sought the help of a therapist, and I stopped putting my head down the toilet.

***

The first divorce hearing came in May. We were summoned. We needed to be there, to appear in front of the judge. Not going wasn't an option, or we stood to lose the money my parents had paid for the proceedings.

The case was to be heard at nine in the morning. I was there fifteen minutes before. By ten past nine, there was still no sign of Bill. The Court Secretary came and asked me how long he would be. I called him.

"I'm lost' was the excuse. "I'm walking around the town, I can't find the Court House."

"You didn't think to look on a map?"

"Of course I did, but I'm on foot. I'm on my way. Will he wait?" Technically, they're not supposed to wait, but I pleaded with the Judge. He could tell I was desperate, and he took pity on me.

At quarter to ten, Bill finally turned up.

"Not too late, am I?"

"Thankfully, no."

We both spent time with the Judge individually, and then we were called in together.

"Mrs Tate. Your husband has expressed a concern that he thinks the amount of alimony paid to you and the children is too much."

I could feel the heat rising in my body. My mouth went dry. I stared at the Judge, and then looked at Bill, who was smugly looking at me.

"I don't understand why," was my reply.

"Get a job," Bill said.

"And the children?"

"Get a full time job, and I'll look after the children." He was still smiling smugly. I thought I might faint. Despite all my resolutions about being able to stand up to him, this had caught me unawares. I had no answer.

"Mr Tate, looking at your current salary, I don't see that your wife is asking for too much. The children are still very young, and her earning power is not as high as yours. I don't think what you are suggesting is either sensible or viable. She will be paying fifty percent of the debt out of this money. She has four mouths to feed; you only have one. You signed the agreement for this amount, and I will therefore uphold it. I will now grant an official separation, and the divorce should be final in three months. Good day to you both."

I exhaled. Thank goodness for that. But what the hell had Bill just tried to do? I could barely look at him. I hated his guts.

Since moving away from the marital home, he'd already found three feeble excuses not to take the kids on weekends he was supposed to have them. There had been a 'business trip' and 'no money to feed them'. On one occasion I'd provided the food myself: some pasta and milk; hardly expensive stuff. But I was getting tired of the excuses now. It was all getting so transparent. And I was starting to see that what he was doing was for the best. He was withdrawing, and I wanted him to.

The information I had exchanged with Richard had given me the strength to stand up to Bill at last. I was no longer a form of narcissistic supply. I was no use to him now, and this was why he was retreating. It was all becoming clear. My life needed to get some direction now, and that direction had to be away from this man. He needed to be out of our lives. However hard it was going to be for me to struggle through this alone with the kids. Struggle through I would have to. I was not going to stand by and let him destroy our lives any more than he already had. He would not mess around with my children's minds, as he had with mine. They deserved better, and I was going to make sure I did all I could to protect them from now on.

I felt fire in my belly for the first time in years. I felt ready to take him on. And win.

Chapter Twenty-Four

Waking Up, and Taking Action

I made an appointment to go and see the lawyer alone. I needed him to know the situation I'd been left with, and to advise me of the best course of action.

"This is difficult to believe, Sarah," he said.

"I know," I replied.

"We knew he was mismanaging many things, but that he'd got you into so much of a mess is quite difficult to comprehend. What on earth was he thinking?"

"I believe he lives in his own world."

He nodded.

"You know the accountant never got paid either?" he asked.

"Really? No, I didn't know that. Why did he keep working then?"

"I think he was hoping things might improve. He's cut his losses now though. He won't be bringing court action. He knows there's no point."

"How much is he owed?" I asked.

"Several thousand, Sarah." I sighed.

"I have to ask about the tax," I said. "Did he make some mistake? Or did he tell Bill that he was building up such a hefty set of arrears? Bill accused him of incompetence. He claimed not to have known about the tax, social security and pension debts."

He rolled his eyes and shook his head.

"No, Sarah. Bill knew about it all. He came up with many seemingly plausible excuses as to why it hadn't been paid. He knew about it, though."

I wasn't in the least bit surprised.

"What about the business deal with the trees? Or the brokering of the finance deal with your Russian colleagues?"

Again, he shrugged his shoulders.

"With the trees, we paid him ten grand to give us a risk analysis and business proposition. We waited months, yet received only a piece of A4 paper with a sloppy and ill thought out proposal on it. I took the money back when the builders repaid some of the house deposit. As for the finance deal, he turned up at the meeting in London with no plan from his Swiss client, and then proceeded to talk for an hour about a possible arms deal with an Eastern European company. My clients called me afterwards to ask who on earth it was I'd sent to them. They were incredibly disappointed at his lack of business prowess. That deal was never on the table after that first meeting." I shook my head this time.

"Sarah, you weren't the only one to be taken in. We all thought he spoke the truth. You've learned a hard lesson, but it could have been worse for you. I think I'll be able to get you out of most of this mess, and I won't charge the full rate."

"Thank you so much." I was fighting back the tears.

"You're welcome, Sarah."

I signed Power of Attorney over to the lawyer. He would negotiate me out of as much of Bill's debt as he could. I knew he would do his best for me. There was nothing else I could do from a practical point of view. The kids and I were living in financial limbo, and it was a very scary place to be. During the three month grace period between the divorce hearing and the final decree, the law refused to acknowledge that we were running two households, and made no allowance for myself and the kids when assessing how much of the debt they would forcibly take from Bill's salary each month. His contract was temporary, and despite his usual protestations of how the company couldn't possibly survive without him, it was becoming clear that they most certainly could, and would.

He just about managed to pay the rent, but not once was he able to transfer the agreed amount of living expenses for myself and the kids.

In June, I received a letter from the car leasing company to inform me that the car hadn't been paid for since February. The letter was to notify me that bailiffs would be coming to pick up the vehicle the following week. When I challenged Bill about it, he casually asked me if I hadn't realised that the car needed paying every month.

"Did you think I was paying it?" he asked, seemingly incredulous. I inhaled deeply, I didn't really want to get into this with him; it was becoming so predictable and way too draining on my energy. I knew that the only way I'd get through this with my sanity intact, would be to dismiss this kind of incident, and focus on getting the divorce finalised. I couldn't allow myself to be dragged into any more of his mind games. I was still incredibly fragile.

The children were confused. Tim was too little to be affected by it all, but the girls were unsettled. Lucy seemed to be the worst affected; she began wetting herself. It broke my heart, but I tried to give them all the reassurance and love that I could.

"Why don't we live with daddy anymore?" she asked one day.

"Because mummy and daddy can't live together any more, sweetheart. We still love you very much, but we've stopped loving each other now, and we are better off living apart. We were making each other very unhappy, you see."

"When can we see him again?"

"He's busy right now, but in a couple of weeks he'll have some time; you need to be patient."

I had no idea when he would 'have time' again by this point. His job was about to come to an end, and there was no sign of any more work on the horizon. I wondered if he would ever be successful in getting a job again, given his track record, and the fact that all his money was being seized by the authorities to whom he owed all the back tax. I also wondered about the state of his mental health. In June he'd announced to me that a major computer software company was trying to head hunt him for a job in Tokyo. He had enthused about the amount of money they were offering him, insisting they were going to jet him out to Japan, via Bangkok. He apparently had no money at all at this point, and I found it most odd that any company would pay for a flight halfway around the world upfront, particularly as this particular company had its actual head office in Zürich. He took the trip, then announced the following week that 'some other arsehole' got the job.

I was at the house the week after his trip, only to discover a makeshift Buddhist shrine in his basement office. He'd clearly made it as far as Thailand. Was there an interview? Probably not, but I'll never know now. Once again, it was my parents who kept our heads above water during this period. They were owed thousands by now, and they knew as well as I did that he had no means, nor intention, of ever paying them back. I was barely able to meet the rent by now, and it led to difficulties with the friend whose apartment I was living in. I felt utterly helpless and terrified. I went to the authorities to ask for support. They reassured me that, as soon as the divorce was final, the kids and I would be awarded the designated minimum amount required for a family of four. This would mean moving again, to a more affordable place. This would be the sixth move in five years. I only hoped this would mark the end of all the upheaval.

By the end of July, his contract ended, and there was no sign of any work on the horizon. I was finding it difficult to communicate with him at all anymore. It was getting too tiring, trying to sort out the fact from the fiction. I was still trying to come to terms with the information I'd received from Rich. There was so much to digest, and I was trying to process the emotions that came with the knowledge he'd given me.

"You're strong, Sarah," he'd said to me during one of our now frequent on line chats.

"But I don't feel as though I am. If I were strong, surely I'd have realised my mistake much sooner?"

"You took your marriage vows seriously, you wanted the family to work, you mustn't reproach yourself for that."

But I still did. Despite being armed with the steadfast belief that I could not have prevented what had happened, the guilt remained. Every time I looked at my children, I felt it. I hated what we were putting them through, and despite all the reassurances I was getting from family and friends that I was doing a great job, I still didn't truly believe it. You want to do all you can to protect your children. The thought that you are the cause of their confusion or pain is unbearable. I was trying my best to hold things together for their sakes, but the girls were still witnessing a mother who was constantly on edge and distracted. I felt I was always so preoccupied with trying to sort out the practicalities of our lives, that I had no time to provide them with some peace and joy. I felt they were missing out on family time, and they were certainly missing out on normality. But I didn't know how to provide normality. It was all I could do to get through each day, wondering when the next unpaid invoice would arrive in my letterbox, or how the hell I was going to keep my name out of the courts. The resentment towards Bill was immense at this time. I was no longer able to speak to him directly, instead using short emails to inform him about what was happening. He had made no effort to speak to the lawyer about the debts, nor had he made an effort to contact the Schroders about their loan. He had professed to me that his time would be better spent 'generating income', yet there were no employment prospects in sight. I was left to coordinate the house sale, the debts, the children, and another move. My mind was exploding with all the things going on, and on top of that there was the anger and frustration. Something had to give, and soon.

***

In August, I received an offer on the house. It was for fifty thousand less than we'd paid for it, but the lawyer advised me to accept the offer for a quick sale.

"What about the Schroders?" I'd asked.

"We will have to negotiate with them," came the reply.

"They will lose money, but you can't worry about that, Sarah. The most important thing is that you get the house out of your name and the bank is satisfied. I have spoken to them, and they will wipe out the mortgage and maybe the credit card debts if you can finalise the house sale in a couple of months. There are other costs to be paid, including my fee, but I think I can negotiate with the Schroders. I'll remind them that it's this, or bankruptcy. If you go bankrupt, they get nothing."

I was heartbroken. These people had trusted us, and they were about to lose a vast amount of money, because of us. I couldn't face speaking to them. I was so ashamed. The lawyer acted on my behalf. He negotiated them down by seventy-five thousand francs. I can only imagine how they suffered as a result. It makes me feel sick to this day when I think about it. More innocent people dragged into this mess. And did he have a conscience about them? If he did, it didn't show.

The second to last time I saw Bill, was when I went to the house to collect some more belongings of the kids, and mine before it was sold. I had emailed to let him know I'd be coming, and to ask him to gather anything he could find of mine and the kids. He had told me he'd arranged some temporary accommodation in Zürich, but that he would be unable to take the kids' belongings, as there would be no room.

The boxes were piled in the living room of the house when I arrived. As I loaded things into the car, he spoke about his employment prospects; about who was desperate to employ him next, and about how confident he was that things would improve soon. His words were animated; his body language was not. I looked into his eyes, and saw nothing. His insincerity was overwhelming. Oh, how my eyes had been opened by now. I couldn't even bring myself to feel pity for the man.

When I got home, I put the boxes into the cellar of the apartment. Before doing so, I had a quick look to see he had included all the kids' belongings. I was shocked to see how the toys had been thrown into the box, like rubbish into the bin. Lucy had a toy Princess Castle. It had been her fourth birthday present from Bill and me. She had loved it. It had been thrown into the box in pieces. Small parts were rattling around loose at the bottom. I was appalled. How could he? And there were drawings. Pictures they had done for him, with 'Daddy' written on them. They too had been thrown into the box. It was as though he'd just removed all trace.

I tried to reason his motives for doing this, and to this day I don't believe it was out of a complete lack of feeling for them. Instead, I prefer to believe that it was a wholly selfish act on his part, and that he needed to remove these items from his life, because he couldn't bear to be reminded of what he had lost. The alternative is too much for me to contemplate, even now. So I will continue to believe my own theory. The man was consumed only with himself and his own problems. He was removing his children as an act of selfish self-preservation, and not because he didn't care about them, surely.

The next time he called though, I could barely contain my distain.

"I'll be moving next week. I'll leave the keys inside the house. I'll be in touch when I'm sorted," he'd said.

"You do that. Don't bother getting in touch until you've got some concrete news Bill. Don't bother calling me with feeble excuses about not having money to feed our kids. Don't call me with bullshit stories about new job prospects and making millions. Don't try to offer me 'cash under the table,' it's all nonsense, and you know it. I've heard it all now. I've been working through the mess you left me with. I've done everything single-handedly, without one ounce of support from you. I think I can now safely say I don't need you for anything. The divorce is final as from next week, and I will get money from the Government from now on until I can find a job. You don't need to pay anything to me anymore. Everything will go via the official channels from now on. You only need to think about yourself now. It shouldn't be too difficult for you. There is no need to even consider us. I've taken care of the kids and myself. Get in touch again when you've sorted yourself out."

And so it was left, for weeks on end. I didn't hear a word from him. When I got the divorce papers through, I took them to the authorities and organised financial support. I found a new apartment for us all, and began to plan the next move. I waded through the mountain of unpaid bills, and dealt with what I could. I wrote begging letters to the authorities about my half of the tax, to the credit card companies, the pension fund, insurances, and even the cable television bill from the house I hadn't lived in for the last six months.

I busied myself with the children, giving them all the time and love I could manage. I tried to put him out of my mind, and not to think about what he might be doing or how he might be feeling. When the children asked about his whereabouts, I tried to answer them in the most honest way I could. I explained that daddy had some problems that he needed to sort out, and that he'd be in touch again as soon as he could. Time went by, and there was still no word. Niggling doubts began to creep back in. Had I done the right thing? It was right for me, but was it right for the kids? How on earth could he go this long without seeing them or even speaking to them? How was I supposed to explain this to them? The girls were hurting. They were confused and bewildered. I felt so helpless, and so very, very angry with Bill.

Eventually, after twelve weeks silence, I could take it no more. I spoke to the authorities, but they seemed to have no idea where he was either. He hadn't been picking up his registered post at the address he'd given to them. In the end, I called his one and only friend I knew, to see if he'd heard anything. I got a frosty reception to say the least. I was told he didn't know where he was. Ten minutes later though, I got a call from Bill.

"You're looking for me? What do you want?" he said.

What did I want? He hadn't been in touch for twelve weeks, and he's asking me what I want? I was flabbergasted. But it made me think. What did I actually want? Why had I bothered trying to track him down? What would it achieve?

"You told me not to contact you until I was sorted. So I haven't." It was a fair enough response, I reasoned.

"OK, do you want to see the children?" I asked.

"Of course I do, you know I do."

"It's just that you've got a strange way of showing it. It's been three months with no word. What do you think I'm supposed to say to them?"

"I was pretty sure you're dealing with it OK. For what it's worth, I think you're doing a good job."

How the hell did he know if I was doing a good job or not? He had no contact with any of us. He didn't have a clue how I was, or how the kids were doing. Why the hell had I bothered contacting him? My blood pressure was rising again. Every contact I had with him now left me feeling more and more angry and frustrated. Just speaking to him seemed to de-rail me. I couldn't afford to let this happen anymore!

"I just wanted to let you know that I've applied for sole custody of the kids. It won't change your visitation rights, but as the divorce agreement states we have shared custody, and you now live so far away, I can't see the point."

There was silence on the other end of the phone.

"Fine," he said eventually.

For me, it was clear after that last conversation. I knew what I needed to do now. It would be the final step. The children needed to be protected. I was not going to allow him to be one of those fathers who would drift in and out of their lives at whim.

There was one more meeting. I arranged to take the kids into town so he could treat them to a McDonalds. I would wait in the café next door for an hour, and then bring them home again. It was emotional. We both knew this would probably be the last time. I thought I saw pain in his eyes, and tears, real tears. I wondered what thoughts went through his mind that day. I wondered if he realised that what was happening was for the best. We were both letting go. I knew it was for the best, but it was still incredibly hard. These innocent children were at the centre of this. They had no idea what was going on. They sensed and saw the pain in him, and in me. They couldn't explain it, and they wept afterwards, as I did. We held each other close that night, the four of us. This was the end.

In the New Year, I was summoned to appear in court for the custody hearing. I had written a long and detailed letter to the judge, explaining my reasons for wanting sole custody, and had also made it clear to the authorities that I wanted to restrict future access, at least until he'd proven that he could be trustworthy. He didn't show up to the hearing, and custody was awarded to me. Visitation rights remained in place, but since then there has never been an attempt from him to exercise them.

This was the start of a new road for the children and me. It was a road which was heading in a completely different direction. I had never planned to set out on this road. It was not what I'd wanted for the kids or me, but I knew it was a road I would now have to take. The end of the marriage, the end of the lies, the end of the deceit signalled the beginning of a new life. This new life was about regaining control, and coming to terms with what had happened.

The challenges I have faced as a single mother with no income have been immense. There were to be many more tears along the way. But slowly, I've learned how to come to terms with what happened, and coming to terms with it opens the door for recovery.

It's true what they say about time being a great healer, time and distance. If Bill had chosen to remain in our lives, I may well not be in the position I am now. I sincerely doubt I could have begun on the road to recovery quite so soon. The fact that I no longer have to deal with his presence has been of huge benefit to the kids and me. In order to recover fully from this type of abuse, you need to be able to understand what it is. I'd never heard of Narcissistic Personality Disorder, or Anti-social Personality Disorder, until I came across an article on it quite by chance, over a year after my divorce became final. Reading about this, and related personality disorders, made me feel as though a light had suddenly been switched on. I realised I wasn't the first person this has happened to, and I would most certainly not be the last.

Over year and a half have passed since I last saw Bill. It's been a year and a half of major highs and lows. You can't prepare yourself for how you're going to feel, or cope. You just have to get on with it and make the best of what you have. You come across hurdles you never anticipated, but with each one you gain strength and resolve. There have been some dark moments in the last eighteen months, but there have also some been some incredibly proud ones. We're in it together ,me and the kids. It's us against the world. I'm still a long way off being completely recovered. I'm not over the anger, and I'm certainly not over my own guilt. I've had to take a long, hard look at myself, and understand how, if at all, I contributed to his pattern of behaviour. Narcissists and sociopaths can only operate successfully when they have a source of supply. You, as that source, need to understand your role, and make a conscious effort to break free. Only then can you start to recover. I have spent a lot of time feeling bitter, but as we all know, these negative emotions lead nowhere. They just drain us, and impact on our ability to overcome the abuse. The key to successful recovery lies in the letting go. It's incredibly hard to let go of all the pain and anger. It takes strength and courage to rise above it all and move on. But it must be done.

I still have a long road to travel before full recovery is reached, but I can see when I look back just how far I've come. I'm proud of what I've achieved so far, and I fully intend to keep on plodding down this road, because it's the road to freedom, for my children, and for me.

Thank You

I want to thank you now, from the bottom of my heart,
Not for the pain you caused, or the lives you've torn apart,
I want to thank you now, for the person you've become,
You've accepted what you are, that you'll never be someone,
The pain has grasped you now, biting deep within your soul,
Nothing you could do now could replace the lives you stole,
You are a fading shadow, of a life which went to waste,
All those opportunities, can never be replaced,
You think you have it in you, the love you clearly seek,
Yet you could never reach it, for that part of you is weak,
You believed you had a need for it, a capacity to share,
But sadly now, you realise, that gift was never there,
You became consumed in self-deceit, in narcissistic thought,
A life of puerile fantasy, leaving those you touched
distraught,
You tried your best, you think you did, you believe you gave
your all,
But in the end, you brought it down, your pride led to your
fall,
Thank God you left the best with me, I have all I'll ever need,
I'm richer than you'll ever be, I'm tainted not by greed,
You've taught me who I shouldn't be, you've changed my
view of life,
I've recognised my worth, you see, I'm more than some-ones
wife,
And that you've chosen now to go, and live your life your
way,
It's for the best, you know it too, that's all that I can say,
You are not able to provide the things we want or need,
You're not a man who's capable of helping us succeed,

285

That task is mine and mine alone, you know you lack the strength,
The choice you made was wholly right, to keep us at arm's length,
I see the wisdom in your thoughts, the reason why you chose,
To leave us all behind at last, and draw this to its close,
The choice you made is best for us, your one last saving grace,
You recognised we're better off, if you vanish without trace,
You know you are not worthy of the gifts that you received,
The lives you once destroyed, the other people you deceived,
And so, I thank you now, I do, though others find it strange,
They think it odd, you see, how my attitude has changed,
But I have learned you must forgive, the ones you should detest,
So I free myself, forgive you now, and wish you all the best,

The End

Comment on 'Web of Lies – My Life with a Narcissist'

Dr David A Holmes
Senior Lecturer in Psychology
Director of the Forensic Research Group
Dept Psychology
Manchester Metropolitan University

During my many years immersed in forensic and clinical psychology, I have always emphasised the importance of real life case histories to the true understanding of dangerously disordered individuals. Being able to see their behaviour and thinking played out in the context of daily life enables untrained individuals to become slowly aware of the uneasy seam between their reality and our own. This is rarely more important than it is in the case of individuals who are what is termed Cluster B personality disordered or even in those whose personality distortions are just below the level of clinical diagnosis making them less salient but still dangerously dysfunctional. Often the devil is literally hidden in the detail of the reactions and behaviour of such individuals, as the inevitable trail of chaos and harm builds in the wake of these self-serving sharks as they serially manipulate their innocent victims. The concept of personality assumes that we have a robust and unchanging way of dealing with the world as we move from situation to situation.

Some 'situationists' have argued that we are different people in different contexts with chameleon-like changes to our reactions. However, the evidence for stable personality traits throughout our lives and situations is overwhelming. In the

287

case of personality disorders, personality traits are very strong and highly resistant to change to the point of causing distress and undermining the ability to function normally in occupational and social contexts. Personality disorders can have a profoundly damaging effect on relationships, to the extent that personal relationship problems are viewed as the 'litmus test' for disorders in the participants. The damage within personal relationships can be very serious with what are termed the Cluster B disorders, which include antisocial personality disorder, borderline personality disorder, histrionic personality disorder and narcissistic personality disorder. With this group of disorders, distress and suffering tends to be endured by those in contact with the disordered, not the personality disordered individual themselves. There is normally remarkable overlap between the different personality disorders with most sufferers qualifying for two or more personality disorder diagnoses at the same time, although more often than not these are from the same cluster. Although, personality disorders as a whole are common at just over 10% of the general population, Cluster B disorders are rarer, but account for a large proportion of the prison population. Fortunately, narcissistic personality disorder is possibly the rarest of these.

As the name suggests, individuals with this disorder are highly self-centred, having an unrealistically high opinion of themselves and their status, a pervasive and persistent grandiosity in all areas of their lives and is not simply showing off to a few friends. They require constant attention and compliments, but lack genuine empathy for others and thus select acquaintances on the basis of utility or attentiveness and exploit them without consideration for the other's feelings or welfare.

Thinking they can only relate to people with high status, which is how they see themselves, and ignore those they perceive as ordinary. Narcissists will fabricate their lives and lie continually in order to maintain false status. Most of those with personality disorders know their behaviour is odd but narcissistic individuals lack insight and are surprised if they fail to get special treatment, attention or praise. They are self-obsessed and devalue the achievements of others against their own as well as having a serious lack of empathy that is highly destructive to any relationships they may have, which also suffer from their jealousy and an arrogant sense that they deserve superior treatment at all times, based on their self-proclaimed uniqueness. A bizarre sense of entitlement can lead to usurping the recognition of others or even their possessions accompanied by aloof arrogance and snobbishness towards others, including friends. Very sensitive to criticism of themselves, they will retaliate with rage or a false humility to protect their pride. Narcissistic rage can and has led to homicide.

Elements of this disorder are woven into the character portrayed in this book with aspects of another personality state also familiar to forensic psychologists, psychopathy. Many psychopathic individuals have superficial charm and lack the 'emotional baggage' of more sensitive people, making the psychopath socially attractive in the short term. Having disarmed potential victims with 'charm', they will proceed to entertain themselves by manipulating their prey to gain what they want, be that material, sexual or sadistic satisfaction. Having indifference to the actual feelings of others, but an acute intellectual awareness of the effects of their manipulation or intimidation, gives psychopaths a predatory advantage over other criminals as well as the many innocent victims. In 1835, Pritchard's use of the phrase 'moral insanity' was as apt as the later book title by Cleckley 'the mask of sanity' in capturing the nature of psychopathy.

In courtrooms, 'not being of good character' tends to refer to the personality disorders described above. However, the more dangerous personality disordered individual is unlikely to come to the attention of clinicians by asking for treatment. It is only when their behaviour results in criminal charges that they enter the clinical forensic radar, usually as prisoners. This is inevitably too late for the poor individuals sucked up into their world who may suffer for many years unable to comprehend what is wrong with their relationship until desperation forces escape for the lucky. Thus, it is up to those many innocent and often generous victims to recognise their situation in order to pull the escape chord. Real-life examples such as that contained in this book can reach in to these situations and perhaps avoid human suffering.

Many of the aspects of what is now termed dangerous and severe personality disorder (DSPD) are evident in the pages of this book, from the characteristic disregard for the truth, law and feelings of others, to dismissal of the rights of those standing in his way. It may not be necessary to meet the full criteria for narcissistic personality disorder or psychopathy in order to wreck the lives of others, but it is vital that potential victims are very aware of all of these warning signs.

Acknowledgements

Thank you so very much to all the dear friends who have encouraged me to write this book. You don't know how much it means to me that you believed I could do this. To all those who stood by me through the really dark times (you know who you are),I am forever in your debt. All the way through, I've felt truly humbled that so many people showed us their love and support. I hope you all know how much I appreciate it. A very special thanks to Brooke and Anne. You are as much a part of this book as I am.

And finally, to Mum and Dad. Without you, none of this would have been possible. You were there for me when I thought there was no way out. It was your love and generosity which got us through this. We are forever in your debt. Love and hugs to you both xxx

Note: The song Lyrics *'Words'* are inspired by the 1992 Madonna song of the same name.

About the Author

Sarah Tate is a single mother living and working in Switzerland. She arrived in Switzerland ten years ago and apart from a brief stay in France, has remained ever since, as Switzerland has become her adopted homeland. Sarah has three young children, who take up most of her time, but she still managed to find time to write her first book 'Web of Lies - My life with a Narcissist'. Her second book, Renaissance – A Journal of Discovery' will be published in early 2011. It describes the road to recovery from narcissistic abuse, and charts the progress of Sarah and her children as they rebuild their lives following the break-up of the family, and slowly come to terms with the devastation caused by Sarah's ex.

CPSIA information can be obtained at www.ICGtesting.com
Printed in the USA
BVOW041329040912

299539BV00017B/60/P